INVESTING IN
EQUITY
OPPORTUNITY
& OUR COMMUNITY
cicf.org

Praise for *From Generosity to Justice*

"Orchestrating a dynamic chorus of vital voices and vibrant vision, Walker harnesses singular storytelling to catalyze ideas and instigate inspiration for a more just future."
—Ava Duvernay

"*From Generosity to Justice* is a rare, eye-opening, and exciting read that opens both the heart and mind."
—Shonda Rhimes

"This will become a defining manifesto of our era."
—Walter Isaacson

"Walker bravely tackles the subject of inequality with one pressing question in mind: What can philanthropy do about it?"
—Ken Chenault

"A recalibration and reimagination of the philanthropic model crafted by the Carnegie and Rockefeller families over a century ago. This new gospel must be heard all over the world!"
—David Rockefeller, Jr.

"Walker illustrates how philanthropy is about more than giving money away; it's about giving energy, and providing 'righteous optimism' for the sake of justice."
—Agnes Gund

"A clarion call for a new kind of philanthropy to transform our society."
—Joel Fleishman

"His bold call for business leaders to demonstrate moral courage is just one part of a new model for justice-minded philanthropy, one that offers both the advantaged and disadvantaged tangible ways to disrupt inequality."
—Indra Nooyi

"*From Generosity to Justice* shows why Darren Walker is one of philanthropy's most forward-thinking and important leaders."
—Michael Bloomberg

FROM GENEROSITY TO JUSTICE

FROM GENEROSITY TO JUSTICE

A NEW GOSPEL OF WEALTH

DARREN WALKER

DISRUPTION
BOOKS

New York   *Austin*

Published by The Ford Foundation / Disruption Books
New York, NY
www.fordfoundation.org
www.disruptionbooks.com

For ordering information or special discounts for bulk purchases, please contact
Disruption Books at info@disruptionbooks.com.

Cover and text design by Sheila Parr

Library of Congress Cataloging-in-Publication Data available

978-1-63331-077-3
eBook ISBN: 978-1-63331-078-0

22 23 24 25 26 27 28 29   10 9 8 7 6 5 4 3 2 1

*For David, who taught me the meaning
of generosity, justice, and love.*

CONTENTS

FROM
GENEROSITY
TO
JUSTICE

PREFACE

In January 2020, I wrote a New Year's message reflecting on what I called "the hard work of hope." I anticipated a difficult year ahead.

At that moment, inequality had reached staggering, all-time highs, all around the world. As I described in the *New York Times*, many well-intentioned friends would deliver soliloquies about dazzling economic growth, at home and abroad. But what I knew, informed by my own life's journey, was that the social-mobility escalator had ground to a halt, setting in place an inescapable, insidious hopelessness that had begun to asphyxiate democratic values and institutions. With many millions teetering on an economic precipice, the anxiety, resentment, and grievances were gathering—and the forces exploiting this insecurity were sure to respond with increasing mendacity and impunity.

I asked rhetorically, then, "What *new* crisis needs to befall us before we, together, are spurred to collective action?" If we weren't moved to organize and mobilize for justice after the turbulent first two decades of the twenty-first century—after all that we had endured—would we ever be?

Little did I imagine.

For several weeks, a novel coronavirus had been spreading across Asia and Europe. The very same day I shared my New Year's essay, in fact, the Centers for Disease Control and Prevention reported the first confirmed case of Covid-19 in the United States.

And then, everything changed. To paraphrase Ernest Hemingway, it happened slowly, then all at once.

The same March week that Americans closed schools and offices—canceling competitions and performances—police officers in Louisville shot and killed Breonna Taylor in her own home. As the virus raged that spring, George Floyd was murdered by a Minneapolis police officer, with untold billions of people watching on televisions, tablets, and smartphones around the globe.

Many took to the streets, demanding an overdue reckoning with our nation's history and legacy of racism—not only in America's criminal-justice and mass-incarceration systems, but, as significantly, in our classrooms and workplaces, throughout our culture and society, the world over.

And then, of course, the President of the United States refused to concede a free and fair election. Insurrectionists desecrated the United States Capitol and attempted to overturn the United States Constitution. This was the worst, but hardly the only, effort to disenfranchise on a scale unseen since Jim Crow.

To me, the historic disruption underway is something altogether different in kind, not just degree. I commented in a 2022 opinion essay that our nation seems more irreparably divided than ever before in my lifetime, barreling down a parallel path, perhaps, to the one our forebears traveled in the 1850s.

Our converging crises of extreme inequality, racial injustice, and autocratic, anti-democratic impunity—multiplied not just by each other, but also by a pandemic that has claimed more than 6.5 million lives (and counting)—pose grave peril to our survival, as does a changing climate that is pushing our life-sustaining ecosystems to the brink of collapse. The droughts and floods, the storms and fires, all are worsening. Further, the distortion of our capitalism, and the inequality it continues to produce, have overloaded this burden onto the backs of the poor, the marginalized, and the vulnerable.

We are staring down existential risk—and as a global and national community, our window to act is closing. If we *only* do what we've always done, the trauma of these last few years will be *only* the beginning.

In this context, philanthropy has, by necessity, initiated a number of bold experiments since the beginning of 2020. For one, we continue our work to treat courageous visionaries on the frontlines of social change with greater respect—as our partners, not our vendors—providing them the resources and flexibility to chart the way forward.

For another, we are using more of our assets more fully—beyond our historic pattern of granting only 5 percent of our endowment value, each year, as required by the United States tax code. At the Ford Foundation, this was the guiding principle behind our $1 billion commitment to mission-related investments, which are proving the potential of capital markets to deliver both a financial and social return. And during the depths of 2020, the same philosophy led us to finance a $1 billion social bond, effectively doubling our payout rate and injecting a capital booster to the organizations meeting our cascading crises. Many of our fellow funders are deploying similar strategies to unlock the power of the other 95 percent.

With *From Generosity to Justice: A New Gospel of Wealth*, I hope to recenter attention and action—across the public sector, business, and civil society—on these approaches and others. After all, the ideas within this book, conceived and championed by a new generation of rising leaders, are demonstrating their mettle under fire.

Ultimately, I feel more strongly than ever that philanthropy is not one kind of action or entity, but rather a continuum that spans from generosity on one side to justice on the other—and that we must push our work, wherever and however we can, beyond the former to the latter.

At the turn of the last century, it was a Chicago muckraker journalist and humorist, Finley Peter Dunne, who coined that most illustrative phrase: "Comfort the afflicted and afflict the comfortable." We must do both, as my friends Elizabeth Alexander and Ken Frazier contend here.

As I see it, "comforting the afflicted" is about our charity, our kindness, our magnanimity—about providing relief and recovery. But "afflicting the comfortable" is about our pursuit of justice—how we reimagine and reform. One asks that we "give something back," but the other insists that we "give something up."

Afflicting the comfortable compels us to recognize the inequalities that make relief both necessary and possible: caste, as Isabel Wilkerson perfectly phrases it; decades of Ayn-Rand, Milton-Friedman, greed-is-good excess; the *conscious* choices that aggregate into a *conscienceless* capitalism. Afflicting the comfortable demands that we reckon with the ways in which we, ourselves, benefit from vast disparities in access and agency, voice and value. And afflicting the comfortable obligates us to rectify—to repair—the deep inequalities that deceive us into ignoring how and why we put ourselves first and others second, resetting the cycles of privilege built into our laws, norms, customs, and behaviors.

All of this constitutes a new gospel of giving, defined by timeless terms and tenets, as I argue in these pages. It calls on us to improve the systems and structures that shaped us, to engage with the root causes of our most urgent crises, not just the immediate consequences, even when those root causes implicate us. It challenges us to trust the people and communities most proximate to problems to shape the most effective solutions to those problems—to value their lived experience as equal to established expertise.

This requires moral leadership and moral courage: that we fix our eyes over the horizon, beyond the next earnings report or the next election, and toward a long-term vision for a more inclusive, equitable society. It also defies us to do something perhaps even harder: to step away from the extremes and from the edge, away from sanctimony and certitude, and to listen and learn with curiosity, and openness, and empathy—with tolerance for one another.

In ordinary times, hope is rare. But in these extraordinary times, hope is *radical*.

And so, I share this book with the radical optimism that we can, and must, and shall overcome. Through our triumphs and our defeats—two steps forward, one step back—we will continue our ascent from truth, to reconciliation, to the fullest measure of justice: absolute equality for all people.

Darren Walker
November 2022

INTRODUCTION

A New Gospel of Wealth

Never before has the world experienced so much inequality.

Thanks to major advances in technology, new entrepreneurs fundamentally transform the way people live and work. But these titans of industry also accumulate wealth on an astounding scale, while the vast majority remain in poverty.[1]

And it's not just economic inequality run rampant: Around the world, there are grand disparities in how people are treated in culture and in politics, who can access education and economic opportunity, and which groups are free to express themselves and participate in a democracy. Even in the most progressive, democratic countries, institutions and systems continue to marginalize and exclude low-income people, women, the disabled, ethnic and religious minorities, Indigenous peoples, people of color, and others.

I am not describing our current moment, though it may sound like it.

Rather, this was the state of the world in 1889, when the American industrialist Andrew Carnegie published the first essay of what we would later refer to as "The Gospel of Wealth." Aptly known as the Gilded Age, this was a time when industrialist tycoons enjoyed lives of unprecedented, unimaginable opulence, while ordinary people endured low wages, dangerous working conditions, and overcrowded, unhealthy living quarters.

Back then, the United States' 4,000 richest families possessed nearly as much wealth as the other 11.6 million American families combined.[2] That level of stark inequality is similar to our own most sobering figures. Today, just the top three richest Americans—not even close to the top 4,000—own about as much wealth collectively as all of the bottom half of the United States combined.[3] Globally, 130 years after Carnegie's gospel, Oxfam reports that the 26 richest individuals control as much wealth as the poorest 3.8 billion—half of the current world population.[4]

There's a reason many have called ours the "New Gilded Age."[5] Indeed, today the problem of inequality is even greater.

Economic inequality is one major form of this current crisis—and the form we hear most about—but once again it is not the only one. We also see rampant, pervasive inequality in politics and government; in culture and creative expression; in education and upward mobility; and—especially—in the prejudicial way that our institutions and systems treat women, people with disabilities, the LGBTQ community, Indigenous communities, people of color, and poor people. These different inequalities both cause one another and are the effects of one another. They are deeply interdependent and intertwined.

These inequalities are not abstract, either. They are experienced every day, by nearly every one of us. A distorted form of capitalism has produced extreme wealth for owners and daily insecurity for workers. Authoritarian leaders have suppressed rights and fomented division, discord, and dysfunction. Fast-moving techno-logical innovations, full of rich potential, are instead used by both groups—the owners and the rulers—to suppress and supplant.

These inequalities reflect the fact that some people have a fuller experience of basic human rights than others do. As a result, these "others" have less access to democracy, social and economic mobility, and their own human dignity.

As the president of a social justice foundation with a mission to strengthen democracy, I have one presiding preoccupation: the staggering threat of inequality. Every day, my colleagues and I ask: What can we do to reduce inequality in all of its forms?

Carnegie's answer to the imbalance of wealth in his times—or perhaps more specifically, the displays of extravagance and indulgence that resulted, and the potential upheaval he feared—was something radical. He wrote that wealthy individuals had a special obligation, while they were still alive, to give "benefactions from which the masses of their fellows will derive lasting advantage, and thus dignify their own lives."[6]

In a word: philanthropy.

Carnegie's ideas fundamentally altered the way the world thought about wealth and giving, and his philosophy has served as the underpinning of American philanthropy and, by extension, of giving around the world.

Since then, much of the work of philanthropy has been undeniably beneficial: Millions of people worldwide have been lifted out of poverty, protected from terrible diseases, provided with social and economic opportunity, and given access to new tools and resources with which to improve their lives.

During the twentieth century, an entire field of institutional philanthropy emerged and flourished in the pattern of Carnegie's mold. Iconic American families—from Rockefeller and Rosen-wald to Mellon and MacArthur—endowed and expanded foundations that built schools and libraries, developed new vaccines, revolutionized agriculture, and advanced human freedom. Since 1990, the number of people living in extreme poverty has gone down by over 1 billion. Since 2000, maternal mortality has decreased in every single country (except the United States).[7] The Ford Foundation—the organization I am honored to lead—has given billions of dollars to support programs ranging from public television in the United States, to microlending in Bangladesh, to the Green Revolution and beyond.

Even if you don't work for a foundation or receive a grant from one, it's very likely that your life has been positively impacted by philanthropy in some way.

I've seen this in my own life. I didn't realize until much later that the Head Start school-readiness program, in which my mother enrolled me when I was five, had emerged from a Ford Foundation–funded pilot program. I was in college before I realized the research that led to Pell Grants was also thanks to private philanthropy. Artists whom I have loved, leaders I have admired, movements I have followed—all have been financed, in ways large and small, by philanthropy.

And yet for all the good philanthropy has accomplished—for all the generous acts of charity it has supported—it is no secret that the enterprise is both a product and a beneficiary of a system that needs reform.

A generation ago, Henry Ford II named philanthropy "a creature of capitalism"—and called on its practitioners to contemplate how, as "one of [our] system's most prominent offspring," philanthropy might help "strengthen and improve its progenitor."[8]

There is no question that the systems and laws that allow foundations to exist—and do so without incurring a high tax burden—are the same systems that have contributed to the massive inequality we see today. Despite the fact that our nation was founded on and promotes democratic ideals, we cannot and do not operate democratically. And philanthropy is not accountable in many of the ways our public sector and other private-sector entities are. This is a contradiction we grapple with regularly: How, as beneficiaries of these undemocratic systems, can we repair those same systems?

It is beyond the capacity of philanthropy to fix our economic and political systems entirely. But I believe that as beneficiaries of the biases and flaws of these systems, holders of wealth and influence today—whether individuals, corporations, or foundations—share an urgent obligation to try.

We must try to listen, even though we may think we know what we're doing, because listening is the only way to learn from those who have actual experience with the problem. We must try to bring on new partners, and collaborate in new ways with people and movements from every walk of life—not just those who have access, privilege, or wealth.

We must try to strengthen democratic institutions, even though we, ourselves, are inherently undemocratic—because the strength and effectiveness of philanthropy's innovations are determined by the strength and effectiveness of those institutions.

And of course, we must encourage a more inclusive form of capitalism, even though our resources are in part the result of biased market systems—because the market will never be free or just if it is not inclusive of all kinds of people, and all kinds of social value beyond quarterly earnings and narrow metrics.

Capitalism does not need to be a winner-take-all system. In fact, capitalism and redistribution often go hand in hand. Just think about the hundreds of billions of dollars that Americans give to charity every year. But we too often forget: There's a difference between inclusive capitalism and capitalism run amok. Inclusive capitalism is a system that provides fair wages and affordable housing, and a grid of common goods such as affordable education and clean air and water—it strives for an environment of meritocracy, not aristocracy. The more level our playing field, the more we can use capitalism's undeniable productive power to unlock better ideas for humankind.

To do all this, we must first recognize and reckon with the fact that philanthropy is by no means immune from the plague of inequality—even if that fact makes donors and grant-makers uneasy. If we are to be legitimate participants in the fight against inequality, there is an urgency to our embracing this uncomfortable truth.

Recently, a number of journalists, academics, and commentators have offered insightful, and sometimes incisive, critiques of philanthropy as an enterprise—among them, Anand Giridharadas, Edgar Villanueva, and Rob Reich. While I may not agree with aspects of these assessments, in the aggregate, they raise valid, valuable, substantive concerns. Many have pointed to the ways philanthropy replicates the worst dynamics and inequalities of our broader society.

Each of these criticisms highlights a very real danger: The way we work can easily mirror the imperfect systems that created us, and can perpetuate injustice rather than remedy it. For example, we recognize that our relationship to our grantees—even our grantees working to strengthen democracy—is potentially undemocratic. With our money comes an imbalance of power, which frankly will be difficult to completely erase. The problems—the deepest problems built into our systems, which we understand better than ever before—have not gone away.

And so again, we are left asking the question: *What can we do about it?*

I believe the answer is that we must move beyond generosity and direct our sights—and our work—toward *justice*.

Now is the time for a bolder vision of philanthropy, one that improves itself and the societies of which we are members. And now is the time when philanthropy should include and listen to more voices, perspectives, and people—because as powerful as philanthropy has been, and as wonderful as *generosity* is, we have an even bigger obligation to deliver *justice*.

I've been thinking about this idea for some time. Toward the end of 2015, in *The New York Times*, I first outlined a new charter for philanthropy—a Gospel of Wealth for the twenty-first century. More than a return to Carnegie, this was an invitation for more people to see themselves as part of the project of philanthropy. Whether you lead a legacy foundation or are new to wealth, a member of civil society or a leader of a corporation, someone developing policy or someone without much wealth or privilege at all, there is a place for you to contribute in this New Gospel.

But you might be wondering: What does it mean to move beyond generosity and toward justice?

I see it like this: If bringing canned goods to a food bank to help feed people in the community is a kind of charity—and if advocating for food stamps, free school lunches, and a living wage reflects a deeper kind of social obligation—then dismantling the systems of poverty and oppression that prevent people from being able to afford healthy food in the first place is delivering justice.

If donating to a Kickstarter campaign to support a local artist is a charitable act, then building platforms that support diverse artists and ensure rural communities have high-quality arts programming is further along the spectrum toward justice. Even more just would be building a society that values creativity as much as capital.

If teaching inmates at a local prison is closer to charity, then fighting against the prejudice former inmates face in the working world is closer to justice. And ultimately, the acts that are most just are those that try to dismantle our racist incarceration system altogether.

In short, charity might be writing a check for a cause you believe in, or finding ways to help individuals who have been affected by the scourge of inequality. But justice goes beyond individuals—it's investing your money, time, resources, knowledge, and networks to change the root causes that create the need for charity in the first place.

Advancing justice means addressing systemic issues, not just their symptoms. It means listening carefully to the needs of communities, and giving a platform to the individuals and institutions that are closest to the problems themselves. It means recognizing that we cannot continue to merely ameliorate the conditions caused by capitalism, but must work to strengthen and improve the market system itself—to transform our economy, our society, and our government into structures that work for more people and create equal opportunity for all.

In other words, when we move our work beyond generosity and toward justice, we can make not only meaningful differences in people's lives but also sustainable, structural change to benefit entire communities.

And we've done it before.

Immediately before and after Hurricane Katrina, the people of New Orleans needed help. They needed food and shelter and blankets. They needed clean water to drink, and boats and helicopters to rescue them from flooding. In response, generous Americans stepped into the breach—and collectively offered 330,000 hours of service,[9] over 51 million pounds of food,[10] and $4 billion toward the immediate needs of their fellow citizens.[11] Other countries donated their time, food, and money as well—including 200 women in Uganda, who despite earning just $1.20 a day breaking rocks into gravel, donated $900 to Katrina victims.[12]

These were acts of compassion—and of charity. They were meaningful to the people giving as well as to those receiving—delivering essential support and saving countless lives. But in the weeks and months after the storm, once the world's attention had turned elsewhere, New Orleans faced a new challenge: how to pick up the pieces and start again.

It's easy to forget now, but many at the time didn't even think it was important to rebuild the Crescent City—including the then Speaker of the US House of Representatives.[13] But the city of New Orleans needed to be resurrected, and its people deserved a new home.

When I served at The Rockefeller Foundation, my colleagues and I hoped we could make a contribution to the city's recovery. Thanks to the leadership of too many local leaders, partners, and friends to name here, we provided a $3.5 million grant to help the city organize and implement the Unified New Orleans Plan, which incorporated widespread public participation to create the blueprint for much of the city's redevelopment.[14] And with the help of many of these partners—including the Bush-Clinton Katrina Fund and the Greater New Orleans Foundation[15]—we supported collective action that helped break the bottleneck and make way for a more inclusive plan for development. In fact, in the years since, these very same partnerships have helped bring in hundreds of millions of federal dollars and billions in business investment across the city.[16]

These acts are closer to justice because they go beyond helping immediate needs. Instead, they are acts intended to create new systems and structures that serve the people who depend on them.

Of course, moving toward justice—confronting ourselves and examining the institutions, systems, and structures that benefit us and make up the status quo—will be neither easy nor comfortable. That's why we need to expand our perspectives. It is incumbent upon everyone to ask themselves: *Whom can we include and learn from? Whom can we support and lift up? What can we share based on what we've learned together? How can we work together to achieve this transformation?*

And that is what this book is all about.

After writing about Carnegie and the New Gospel of Wealth in 2015, I heard from people in many parts of the world who were excited and willing to do the work of moving from charity to justice.

The more people with whom I've spoken, the more I've learned about what this process of pushing more of us from generosity to justice will require—and the more connections and resonances I've begun to see among the perspectives of leaders who are running philanthropies old and new, and are on the ground and organizing movements. Everyone should have access to the collective wisdom, guidance, and perspectives of people already doing this work.

This volume is a modest step in gathering the knowledge necessary to move philanthropy along the spectrum from generosity to justice. Here, you'll find a set of tenets that make up a New Gospel of Wealth, which has emerged and been informed by my personal journey and the wisdom I've learned from others in two decades in philanthropy. (And you'll see excerpts from conversations with those friends—and a few conversations in full—throughout this volume.) Together, we will explore how to:

- Recognize the privilege of perspective by seeing and sharing access and opportunity;

- Adopt the awareness of ignorance by learning what we don't know;

- Take ownership of selflessness by giving with humility;

- Work to raise the roots by addressing causes, not consequences;

- Harness the power of proximity by valuing both expertise and experience;

- Exercise the courage of conviction by standing up and speaking out; and

- Promote the democracy of justice by recognizing that our liberation is bound together.

But first, we will examine a continuum of awareness and action—a spectrum that spans from generosity to justice.

As you read these pages, please consider these words to be an open invitation—an extended hand and an opportunity to learn, to grow, to get comfortable with being uncomfortable, and to become better. Whether you are new to philanthropy, or looking for new ways to achieve justice in your work, I hope you will find insight and inspiration.

1

FROM GENEROSITY TO JUSTICE

A CONTINUUM OF PHILANTHROPY

Overcoming poverty is not a gesture of charity. It is an act of justice.[17]
—*Nelson Mandela*

In 2017, Americans gave more than $410 billion to charity in the United States, setting a new record high for the third year in a row.[18] More impressive still, while corporations and foundations accounted for some of that total, the vast majority came from individuals.

For many Americans, this kind of generosity is simply part of our character. Throughout the year, millions of us volunteer at homeless shelters, donate to clothing and food drives, and support relief efforts in the face of devastating natural disasters. Americans are a remarkably bighearted people—yet we do ourselves and our society a disservice if we do not inform these everyday acts of generosity with an equal commitment to justice.

Most of us, understandably, don't think about our individual giving in these terms. When we write a check or slip a bill into a donation box, we aren't thinking about the finer differences between charity and justice. Instead, we put our faith in the organizations we're supporting—trusting that they will spend our money thoughtfully and compassionately.

In this sense, charity is easy: a simple way to feel as though we are doing good. But that same comfort can also allow us to turn a blind eye to the underlying inequities that create the need for charity in the first place.

For most people, charity is an act. But in philanthropy, it can also be a *mindset*—located on one end of the spectrum from generosity to justice. In the decades I've spent working for non-profits and foundations, I've seen the shortcomings of this charity mindset firsthand.

Indeed, many of us realize this charity mindset is insufficient. At its core, it focuses on the immediate. It's limited to alleviating the short-term symptoms of inequality rather than addressing the root causes. And in philanthropy, the charity mindset can perpetuate a power dynamic that privileges the wishes and world view of those who are giving over the lived experience of those who are receiving. Some have even called this mode "transactional."

There are flashes of such condescension in the original "The Gospel of Wealth," in which Andrew Carnegie argues that the wealthy themselves know best how to spend their resources to benefit others. To him, the wealthy man is "agent and trustee for his poorer brethren, bringing to their service his superior wisdom, experience, and ability to administer, doing for them better than they would or could do for themselves."[19]

Today, it would likely be difficult to find a philanthropist who would say these words. But the same arrogance that underpins Carnegie's argument lives on in other, less explicit forms. Despite our good intentions, legacy foundations, as well as newly minted billionaire philanthropists, can easily mistake their power and privilege for "superior wisdom, experience, and ability to administer." As a result, too often philanthropies treat their grantees—many of whom are the people and groups closest to the problems we seek to solve—as contract workers rather than partners. Communities we serve get our support without necessarily getting a role in the decision-making or even a seat at the table.

When we approach giving in this limited way, we diminish the very people we aim to help, and end up reinforcing the inequalities we hope to change. We keep the power to decide and finance an agenda in the hands of very few, rather than including the perspectives of those who have been historically unrepresented or immediately impacted. In other words, if we offer only charity, we fail to address the fundamental injustices in our society. We do nothing to transfer power back to the disempowered communities we claim to serve.

To shift our mindset toward justice, we must also shift our attention.

In this conversation about shifting philanthropy's mindset, while it's easy to focus on those who give, the distinction is easier to see when we focus on those we serve and put them first. Communities in need intuitively understand the difference between charity and justice, and they often organize around and fight for the latter, because it is the more sustainable remedy to structural inequality. Put another way: When was the last time you heard an activist shouting, "No *charity*, no peace"?

When we try to find other people's solutions, we inevitably cause new problems. Our intent and our impact are simply misaligned. That's why we have to be mindful to engage with the community. That's the difference between approaching philanthropy from a charity mindset and approaching it with a justice mindset.

—CARLY HARE, COALITION DIRECTOR OF CHANGE PHILANTHROPY

There is so much we can learn about a justice mindset from those living and working on the front lines, fighting for justice every day. Ikal Angelei is an environmental justice leader in Kenya who has taken up the causes impacting Lake Turkana Basin, where she was raised and now lives. In 2008, Ikal began a campaign against the construction of the Gilgel Gibe III Dam, a project of the Ethiopian government. The dam was meant to generate hydroelectric power for the government to sell to other countries such as Kenya, Sudan, and Djibouti, but the government began the dam project without soliciting any input from the local Indigenous communities—or even notifying them.

When Ikal found out, she was outraged. If the dam was completed, the communities surrounding Lake Turkana stood to lose a valuable water supply. Ecosystems would be uprooted, pastoralists and fishers would lose their livelihoods overnight, and water scarcity could put the entire region in even greater danger of armed conflict and terrorism.

In response, Ikal created a group called Friends of Lake Turkana, uniting the region's divided local communities to fight against the dam. She secured the support of local elders and chiefs, the Kenyan Parliament, and the United Nations. She even convinced the World Bank, the European Investment Bank, and the African Development Bank to withdraw their financial support for the project.

Although it was led by the Ethiopian government, the Gilgel Gibe III Dam has much in common with the kinds of charity-focused international development projects that philanthropies have supported for decades. Ostensibly, such projects are designed with the intention of bringing energy, resources, and jobs to the regions in question and thus stimulating local economies. But when they aren't implemented carefully, these projects can do more harm than good—reflecting and even deepening some of the most entrenched inequalities that marginalized communities already face.

A charitable response aimed at helping the people of Lake Turkana might have looked very different from Ikal's efforts. One can easily imagine a well-meaning philanthropist supplying food and water to the Indigenous communities in the area, intending to offset the disruption to their ecosystem—a short-term intervention that would address a real need created by an even larger injustice. But Ikal didn't want to simply address the symptoms of injustice. So, she dedicated herself to solving the underlying problem.

Ikal's work is a model for what philanthropy can and should support.

Pushing ourselves beyond a charity mindset, and along the spectrum from generosity to justice, also requires understanding how the current unjust system benefits us—and being willing to implicate ourselves.

Understanding that the system is broken is perhaps the easy part. Even Carnegie recognized that inequality was a by-product of the way our societies, markets, and institutions are organized—a fact that we still agree with and see in practice. At the same time, Carnegie believed that our society was, however imperfect, a meritocracy—that the men who accumulated vast wealth were simply endowed with more talent, skill, and intelligence than others. By taking as his premise "that the present laws of competition, accumulation, and distribution are the best obtainable conditions,"[20] Carnegie (along with many of his peers) excused himself from interrogating the root causes of the very inequality he sought to ameliorate.

That's why it is impossible for philanthropists to shift their mindset and their work toward justice without acknowledging that their means to do so—the vast sums of personal wealth that endow so many foundations—is often itself the product of injustice.

> Justice is an unalloyed good. It is an end in itself, and every right-thinking person should be a seeker of justice, unambiguously and unequivocally.
>
> —NICK HANAUER, SEATTLE ENTREPRENEUR AND PHILANTHROPIST, CO-FOUNDER OF THE VENTURE CAPITAL FIRM SECOND AVENUE PARTNERS

The inescapable reality is that many people don't experience society as a meritocracy. For these individuals, the entrenched injustices of our politics, economy, and culture limit opportunity and perpetuate suffering. And yet by gaining an understanding of these systemic injustices—and their relationship to those systems—passionate social justice activists equip themselves with the tools to make change.

Moving from charity to justice will also mean thinking more deeply, shifting our perspective to consider the implications of every decision, and seeking out the sustainable long-term equitable solution. Unfortunately, a charity mindset often limits our focus—and our impact. We can easily imagine how an act of charity might make a meaningful difference in the short term without precipitating a lasting change. A hot meal might mean a great deal to a hungry family, but it doesn't eliminate food deserts or establish a living wage. A disaster relief fund might help a city recover after a hurricane, but it doesn't change the reality that impoverished areas and minority communities are the most impacted by natural disasters.[21, 22] Writing a check for a cause you believe in might bring you a measure of personal comfort—and it likely does some good—but it doesn't change the systems that make charity necessary in the first place.

Laura Arrillaga-Andreessen has thought a lot about this idea. She's the founder and president of the Laura Arrillaga-Andreessen Foundation, an organization that seeks to improve the efficacy of philanthropy and to elevate, through a number of educational resources, both women in leadership and inclusive leadership. What's more, she has taught classes on philanthropy at the Stanford Graduate School of Business since 2000, is the founder and chairman of both the Silicon Valley Social Venture Fund and the

Stanford Center on Philanthropy and Civil Society, and is the author of the book *Giving 2.0: Transform Your Giving and Our World*. As Laura put it, "If charity is a social palliative, then justice is a social corrective. Charity is about helping people survive. Justice is about helping people thrive."

Philanthropist and former Microsoft CEO Steve Ballmer makes a similar argument. He and his wife, Connie, co-founded Ballmer Group, an organization that seeks to improve economic mobility for impoverished families in the United States. Steve put it this way: "Charity runs out of money. Justice with systemic change does not."

Although these distinctions are important as we begin to evaluate how much further we can move from charity toward justice, many philanthropic institutions today don't think of their work as charity. Many of these institutions still miss the mark by not focusing on changing the systems and structures that create inequality.

Over the past century, foundations like Ford have spent tens of billions of dollars building schools, developing vaccines, revolutionizing agriculture, and advancing freedom. Those efforts have given millions of people opportunities they wouldn't otherwise have had. Philanthropies have fed the hungry, cured diseases, built institutions, and saved lives. Yet for all our efforts, the combined wealth of all the world's foundations, donors, and philanthropists hasn't done enough to change the underlying systems that make our work necessary.

Even for those organizations explicitly concerned with justice, it can be hard to resist the temptation to slip back into the mindset of charity, to reinforce the status quo that gives us our privilege. As the leader of such an organization, I know firsthand how easy it is to miss the forest for the trees—to become distracted by the urgent and lose sight of the greater good.

Of course, none of this is meant to diminish the importance of charity in our society. Charity fills empty stomachs, gives beds to the weary, and brings relief to the communities that need it most. Indeed, charity is a fundamentally human impulse. Laura Arnold, attorney and co-chair of Arnold Ventures in Houston, Texas, offered an important reminder: "I think that there needs to be a place for charity too, because it's part of being human. Charity is one way we can be part of a society and part of a community—part of how we show grace and humility and humanity."

She's right—charity and justice must go hand in hand. There's a reason doctors treat the symptoms as well as the disease.

As a physician, Dr. David Skorton knows this better than most. David served as the secretary of the Smithsonian Institution, and before that was the president of Cornell University, during which time he fundraised $5 billion. As both a fundraiser and a physician, David knows the need for short-term and long-term care. "I look at charity like addressing a symptom in medicine, serving an immediate need," David explained. "Justice, on the other hand, is more like treating the underlying disease, the cause of the symptoms—and in an ideal world, preventing the situation that requires charitable actions in the first place."

From a philanthropic point of view, we need both: short-term support to care for people in need and long-term efforts to change the situations that cause this need in the first place.

Implemented correctly, charity can move us toward justice. After all, as Alice Walton, a philanthropist and the founder and chairwoman of the board of the Crystal Bridges Museum of

American Art in Bentonville, Arkansas, put it: "Charity is an act. Justice is an outcome."

Going forward, we can shift our mindset and turn our impulse toward charity into a more intentional pursuit of justice. To do this, we must shift our attention to the voices of those most affected by injustice, because they are the ones who understand the problems best. They are not objects of charity, but drivers of change. Because justice is inclusive, we must never forget that the project of creating a more just world belongs to us all.

In the end, fostering a world where charity is no longer needed is an all-encompassing endeavor that must be approached from every angle and seen through every available lens. This inter-sectional work won't always be easy, and it will take time. But it all begins with us. We have to make the conscious decision to bend each of our acts of generosity toward justice.

2

THE PRIVILEGE OF PERSPECTIVE

SEEING AND SHARING ACCESS AND OPPORTUNITY

Privilege blinds because it is the nature of privilege to blind.[23]
—*Chimamanda Ngozi Adichie*

Successful people often attribute our successes to what we do. We don't always acknowledge the circumstances that make success possible.

Social psychologists sometimes refer to this tendency as the fundamental attribution error, which was summed up quite succinctly in *Harvard Business Review*: "When we succeed, we're likely to conclude that our talents and our current model or strategy are the reasons. We also give short shrift to the part that environmental factors and random events may have played."[24]

Another word for that set of "environmental factors and random events"—for the circumstances and systemic advantages outside of our control that contribute to or create the conditions for our personal success—is "privilege."

Unfortunately, those of us with privilege often have trouble recognizing it. But if we are to establish a New Gospel of Wealth for philanthropy, our first task must be to understand and make visible the privilege we have—as individuals and as a sector.

One of the most notable writers on this subject is Peggy McIntosh, who in 1988 published the seminal article "White Privilege and Male Privilege: A Personal Account of Coming to See Correspondences Through Work in Women's Studies." In it, she identifies 46 instances from her own life that demonstrate the privilege she experiences almost every day.

The list is startling. It ranges from McIntosh's experiences of the world—both in media and in her neighborhood—to other people's perceptions of her. She sees how white privilege manifests in ordinary ways, at the grocery store and the hairdresser and even in the color of bandages. In one of the most powerful lines of the piece, she writes: "White privilege is like an invisible weightless knapsack of special provisions, assurances, tools, maps, guides, codebooks, passports, visas, clothes, compass, emergency gear, and blank checks."[25]

Privilege, for all of us, is the unique set of tools we have to navigate the world. And understanding the origins of these tools is essential for those of us who seek to make the world better. In a 2014 interview with Joshua Rothman of *The New Yorker,* McIntosh says, "In order to understand the way privilege works, you have to be able to see patterns and systems in social life, but you also have to care about the individual experiences."[26]

So often we talk about white privilege, which is a necessary lens, but not a sufficient one. As McIntosh explains:

Whiteness is just one of the many variables that one can look at, starting with, for example, one's place in the birth order, or your body type, or your athletic abilities, or your relationship to written and spoken words, or your parents' places of origin, or your parents' relationship to education and to English, or what is projected onto your religious or ethnic background. We're all put ahead and behind by the circumstances of our birth. We all have a combination of both. And it changes minute by minute, depending on where we are, who we're seeing, or what we're required to do.[27]

That's why it's useful for all of us to take an inventory of the privilege in our own lives, acknowledging our individual experiences as well as the larger systems at play. We must ask ourselves: *What are the benefits that I take for granted? What am I not thinking about, or worried about, that others in my community and country might confront on a daily basis?*

If I were to offer a piece of advice to other philanthropists, it would be to get, and understand, and make visible their own privilege—and to deal with their privilege so that they can be more self-aware in the aspirations they have for their philanthropy. If you don't get comfortable with the idea that privilege is typically invisible to those of us who possess it, you're not nearly as well equipped to make a difference for society.

—JEFF RAIKES, CO-FOUNDER OF THE RAIKES FOUNDATION

As I reflect now on my own privilege, I realize the list is quite long.

I was privileged to be born in the United States, in a place where even growing up relatively poor means something different from what it means in other parts of the world. I was privileged to be born in a charity hospital, to have a loving mother who worked hard and chose to move us to Texas, where I was surrounded by the love of my sisters and extended family.

I was also born male, and thus I have—in numerous ways, many of which are probably unknown to me—benefited from the ways in which our patriarchal society has placed, and continues to place, different demands on men and women.

I was born without any physical, sensory, or intellectual disabilities—and was able to move freely through and readily access a world built for my body and my senses, rather than struggle to navigate a society that did not account for my specific needs. Again, the privilege is not having to worry, not having to think about some facet of my experience that is easy for me but that potentially excludes someone else.

As a black man, I was privileged to be born in 1959, to grow up after many of the accomplishments of the civil rights movement had been won in courts and written into law. What's more, if I had been born just a few years earlier, I would have missed being a member of the inaugural class of Head Start, which in many ways set the groundwork for my future academic success. I benefited from the pure happenstance that the government funded such a program, and that an organization like the Ford Foundation invested in the research to make it a reality.

I also benefited from individual philanthropists and scholarships along the way, and was privileged to attend (as an in-state student—a Texas privilege) one of the best public universities in the country. I could go on and on and on.

None of these acknowledgments take away from my individual success. Rather, they put my personal accomplishments in a broader social context. For me, they make visible all the work required—from government, business, philanthropy, and individuals—to create the conditions that have allowed me to succeed. These conditions are the result of a series of active and passive choices made by our society.

At the same time, none of these privileges made me totally immune to the forces of inequality in my life. Growing up in the South, I was certainly aware of the way prejudice, discrimination, and racism—the legacy of slavery—impacted my own life and the lives of those around me. I saw many of my cousins, no less promising than me but lacking some of my privileges, end up trapped in the criminal justice system.

This is all to say that privilege impacts our lives in ways that are lasting and continuous and sometimes difficult to fathom. It can inoculate us from certain experiences of inequality without erasing the reality of injustice in other areas of our lives.

And these privileges come in many forms over the course of one's life. I now enjoy privileges because of my current position and the resources and reputation of the Ford Foundation, an institution that existed long before I joined it.

With this in mind, we all have so much to consider—in these broad categories, and in more specific instances I cannot begin to enumerate here—and we must pause to appraise the benefits we take for granted. And we must remember how our privileges can have a compounding effect—how our circumstances can widen or narrow the possibility for, and trajectory of, our entire life.

For example, being born in one place means having access to certain resources or schools, and those schools can open up certain networks and professional opportunities. In some institutions, certain privileges are even codified—like how elite colleges give preference to legacy students, the children of graduates. This unearned advantage is actually systemic; schools rely on legacy admissions to keep a steady stream of donating parents. It's a quid pro quo between the privileged school and the privileged parents, a distorted system of incentives that gives a handful of students the very opportunity that might otherwise extend educational privileges and compounding advantages to other families.

Yes, privilege, by its nature, creates the conditions for more privilege.

What's also striking are the ways in which the privileged are tasked with fixing the very system that benefits us. Certainly, privilege exists across philanthropy, but I am glad leaders in the sector are thinking and talking about it, grappling with the responsibility it confers, and considering the need to extend those privileges to others.

David Rockefeller Jr. knows quite a bit about privilege. Along with the Carnegies, the Rockefellers are one of the founding families of American philanthropy, and The Rockefeller Foundation (where I was fortunate to work) has aimed to "promote the well-being of mankind throughout the world"[28] for over a hundred years, tracing its original fortune to the founder of Standard Oil, John D. Rockefeller Sr.—David's great-grandfather. As a result of this wealth, David was able to attend elite schools and dedicate significant energy and time to philanthropy.

Currently, David serves as a trustee for the Rockefeller Brothers Fund, a family foundation started by his father (David Sr.)

and uncles. And thanks to his position, he has spent a great deal of time thinking about what one can do with such privilege:

> *Wealth creators who didn't grow up with privilege are often so engaged in the creation and preservation of wealth that they may not think about all of this as privilege. For those of us who came to it by chance and inherited wealth, it's easier to come to the place of gratitude I feel. I'm just immensely grateful for what my forebears did to create this wealth platform that we're challenged and thrilled to be deciding how to use.*

We cannot change where our privilege comes from, but we can, as David said, decide how to use it. And you don't have to be a Rockefeller to understand privilege or that feeling of gratitude.

Mellody Hobson was raised by a single mother in Chicago, and throughout her childhood experienced the threat and reality of eviction, of not being able to make ends meet. As a black woman, Mellody did not have the advantages of the very forms of privilege Peggy McIntosh first highlighted—white and male—but she was motivated to achieve academic success and financial security. Today, Mellody is the president of Ariel Investments, and she sits on numerous corporate and philanthropic boards, including The Rockefeller Foundation. Said Mellody:

> *I acknowledge that I have this remarkable, miraculous existence— and it's truly a miracle. I'm aware of it every minute of every day. I take nothing for granted. I wake up in the morning and can't believe that I know where I'm sleeping and that I'm not going to be worrying about being evicted, because that was so much of my young life.*

My husband always says what happens to you as a child stays with you in a different way. And because I'm so rooted in that, I'm equally rooted and aware of this privilege that I have. So, I try to do a couple things. One, I try to be aware of it in a way that shows gratitude and humility, as opposed to anything else. Two, I also try to be aware of it in a way that I'm wearing it lightly.

In her approach, Mellody also thinks about her friend Eric Liu, the founder and CEO of Citizen University, who asks the question: *Do you share, or do you hoard?* As Mellody put it, "My goal is to share the privilege."

Sharing privilege might be a first definition of what it means to demand—and deliver on—justice. Sharing privilege requires being aware of the systemic imbalances and going beyond giving resources to consider expanding and altering the current systems of privilege.

This can be a challenge.

"Unfortunately, for many, the privilege leads to a sense of entitlement," Jeff Raikes said. He is the co-founder of the Raikes Foundation, and also was CEO of the Bill & Melinda Gates Foundation after nearly three decades working at Microsoft. He continued, "You might think, 'Because I have this privilege, because I created this wealth, I have the best idea to make a difference for society.' But that's wrong. Instead, you have to turn that around and say, 'I've got to recognize the privilege that I have' and not get sucked into thinking you're entitled to choose what's best for society."

And when we recognize our privilege in all its various forms, we become increasingly aware of our responsibilities. My friend Laura Arrillaga-Andreessen recognizes this. Her father is John

Arrillaga Sr., a man who is credited with building Silicon Valley, and who has participated in a great deal of anonymous philanthropy.[29] Following in those footsteps, she has dedicated her career to service and is the founder of the Silicon Valley Social Venture Fund, the Stanford Center on Philanthropy and Civil Society, and LAAF.org.[30] She described her relationship with privilege insightfully, saying, "I am a white female of extraordinary privilege, and with this privilege I believe I have an even more extraordinary responsibility to use the resources I have and the platform I have created to pursue the work of advancing the lives of others."

"When you have privilege," Laura continued, "you have a responsibility that surpasses your privilege: to use it to effect positive change and to create greater access, greater opportunity, greater empowerment."

This echoes something David Rockefeller Jr. said: "As my grandfather famously put it, 'I believe that every right implies a responsibility; every opportunity, an obligation; every possession, a duty.' And so, it has been my privilege to think about what our responsibility is in the philanthropic realm."

We need not feel guilty for the privileges we identify in our own lives, but acknowledging and understanding them will better ground us for the work to come. If we are to make systemic change, we must deeply understand the systems at play—and how we benefit from them. And for all of us with privilege—of any sort—there is the responsibility to do more. As Carnegie himself wrote:

> It is not the privilege, however, of millionaires alone to work for or aid measures which are certain to benefit the community. Everyone

who has but a small surplus above his moderate wants may share this privilege with his richer brothers, and those without surplus can give at least a part of their time, which is usually as important as funds, and often more so.[31]

Ultimately, privilege should not just create a feeling of gratitude or a moral responsibility; it should also expose us to certain problems, worries, and fears, and give us the power to address them. Our privilege is a tool that gives us access to the resources, networks, and power that we must use to create change and extend these privileges to all. We must not be blind to our privilege, but acknowledge it and wield it for justice.

NEW
PARADIGMS
FOR LEGACY
INSTITUTIONS

—————

1

A Conversation with Elizabeth Alexander

For two years, I was lucky to work with Elizabeth Alexander at the Ford Foundation, where she served as the director of creativity and free expression. In 2018, she was named president of The Andrew W. Mellon Foundation—an organization committed to working in areas such as higher education, the humanities, museums, conservation, and the arts.

The foundation's namesake—Andrew W. Mellon—was born about 20 years after Andrew Carnegie. Mellon was a banker and businessman who amassed considerable wealth and, like Carnegie, benefited from both the industry and the inequality of the Gilded Age. Both men were also philanthropists, motivated to use their vast wealth for the good of society. In fact, they separately founded educational institutions in Pittsburgh that would later merge to become Carnegie Mellon University.

When Elizabeth assumed her role as president of the Mellon Foundation, she brought with her a wealth of knowledge and experience. In addition to a career in philanthropy, Elizabeth is an accomplished academic as well as a celebrated writer of poetry, essays, plays, and memoir. Using her perspective as a teacher and an artist, she has sought to steer her legacy institution toward advocating for education and access for all.

DARREN: When you think about pursuing justice in America and the world, where does philanthropy fit in?

ELIZABETH: When we think about George Soros or Henry Ford or Andrew W. Mellon, they all amassed their wealth in different ways and they all have very different stories. But at the end of the day, the result is still an excess of wealth in one place. What we know is that there can't be an excess in one place if there's not a need in another place. So, I think, at the heart of philanthropy, there are inherently ideas about what wealth redistribution looks like.

Nothing is ever completely balanced, but I do think that this very simple idea—if there is too much someplace, there is a moral obligation to be thoughtful about sharing it—is the central justice idea in philanthropy.

DARREN: Do you see this as simply wealth redistribution for its own sake, or do you see redistribution as addressing the root causes of inequality? John D. Rockefeller, for example, wanted to help black people, but he didn't speak in terms of racial justice. He believed in educating black women, for instance, and his wife's family had long been active in abolitionist movements.[32] So he settled debts at the Atlanta Baptist Female Seminary, a school for black women and girls, and named it after his wife's family— turned it into Spelman Seminary, which became Spelman College, the prominent all-women's historically black college we all know today.[33] But for all that, he never suggested that black women should go to traditionally white women's colleges like Radcliffe or Smith.

ELIZABETH: I think that in our generation, getting at root causes is where the art of philanthropy comes in. Each philanthropy has to figure out and be really intelligent about—and have a higher view on, and have deep knowledge on the staff to be able to really analyze—where it can meaningfully not only make a justice difference (and not everybody can do everything!) but also determine how that idea of justice can have fulsome and visible authorship.

I think that idea of rigorous authorship is very, very crucial, because otherwise good things will happen, money will get spent, people will do their projects—but it won't have any durability or visibility.

DARREN: You're getting at something that philanthropists have been accused of getting wrong: How do we ensure that we empower the people and communities our missions are meant to support?

ELIZABETH: I thought about this a great deal at Ford: How do we, as philanthropists, act as "thought partners" with the people we fund? If we share goals and we have knowledge from all sides, we want to be helpful with more than just a check. But at the same time, we also have to remember whom the work belongs to.

So, to me, that gets back to rigor on staff, and knowing communities deeply so that you can choose grantees carefully. That way, once you've made that choice, you can say, "Okay, we picked you because we trust you. And we don't need to be in constant back-and-forth."

Partnerships can be very fruitful if we remember with humbleness where our expertise lies, and also what we are learning from the people we work with.

That requires humility, but not false humility. I think that's really important to say. It's disingenuous to just say, "Oh, we had nothing to do with this at all." And that gets back to my point about trying to own the authorship of what we do, but in a way that is balanced properly.

DARREN: A lot of philanthropists say our role is really just to be quiet and let the grantees speak for the issues. How do you see the role of using your voice as a philanthropist for justice?

ELIZABETH: I think it is about the discipline of distilling your voice into something that is relatively simple so that the grantees can speak for themselves in all the details. So again, to get back to what you have isolated and what was our guiding principle when I was working for you, I would say to myself, "Every grant must answer the question: Does this disrupt inequality in some way?"

That was hard and interesting, and we would take it through all the channels, and then at the end we could answer that simple question. That was what the Ford Foundation was putting out into the world, and the grantees could exemplify all the details and the particulars and the specifics.

I think similarly with Mellon—and I am still very new in this work, but when I think about the idea behind the Mellon Mays Undergraduate Fellowship Program, for example—it starts with this idea that we believe higher education matters.[34] And if we can articulate the value of why higher education matters, and we recognize that there is not full access to higher education and that the professoriate is not diverse, then there are hundreds and hundreds and hundreds of ways that interesting grants can achieve that wish for excellence and parity.

In this case, the voice of the foundation is saying that excellence and parity in higher education is our value. Then all of these fantastic programs reflect this value in specific ways. I just learned about one we are supporting the other day: Reed College is completely redoing its first-year humanities course so that it will be based not just around the ancient Greeks. They'll still be looking at Athens, but they'll also study Mexico City and Harlem, and in my role, I can just be excited about that. I don't have to imagine that. Instead, I can say it addresses our values, and it's a big and beautiful idea that we believe in.

DARREN: Is that because you believe the role of philanthropy is to help redress, to help lift up? Why are you excited about this idea? Is it because they're including Harlem and Mexico City, and can really compare and contrast cultures? Or is it because they are including something in this canon that has historically been excluded or ignored?

ELIZABETH: I think about the root of the word "philanthropy," from "philo" (to love) and "anthropos" (people). I really carry that as a guide: the animated love of humankind. That is one of the justice drives for me, just thinking about the root of the word and what it means.

But also, I think one of the things that Mellon is devoted to is, again, the value of a higher education, which is no longer a given in this society right now. People are devaluing it to the point where some people question whether it even is meaningful for folks to go to college. So, if we care about higher education, the justice idea is: If an excellent and exquisite education is of value to anyone, it must be available to everyone. If the ideas of groups of people, civilizations of people, countries of people, types of people have been excluded from our collective understanding of the human experience, then as a foundation, we are in favor of work that helps give a more complete picture of where excellence and ideas and felicity have been found throughout history and into the present.

DARREN: It sounds like you're saying forcefully, though, that philanthropy has a role to play in achieving that.

ELIZABETH: Yes, I am saying it forcefully because I do believe that if you love the people, then your excess resources should be used for the betterment of more people.

DARREN: So, when we move from charity to justice, how is that challenged? There are people who would say, "Oh, I love people, but I just want to do charity. I don't want to get uncomfortable, or participate in all of this justice stuff." As you know—from your time here at Ford and in the larger world—the whole pursuit of justice as a philanthropist can make other philanthropists uncomfortable, and make other people uncomfortable. Now, as Congressman John Lewis reminds us, we don't make progress without getting uncomfortable. But philanthropy is not often a sector where people want to really get uncomfortable.

ELIZABETH: That's right. My version of Lewis's comment—my guiding light—is something I remember the poet Lucille Clifton heard from a preacher: "I come to comfort the afflicted and to afflict the comfortable."[35]

It would be contradictory to my whole life to see it any other way, and I'm bringing that into this philanthropy arena. So, I'm not uncomfortable with the discomfort. But this is where, to me, it's really interesting to think about who is in philanthropic leadership right now and what models might actually give us some very powerful tools to help people move through that discomfort.

Part of my career has been teaching socioeconomically, ideologically, and experientially mixed groups of kids—largely white because of the universities where I taught, but crucially, still mixed—about the challenges of African American studies, and having these students confront things that they had not before, learn how to move that racial conversation forward, and see how transformative and productive that is. All the while, they're falling in love with black culture and also learning to write, speak, and analyze with sharp clarity.

I recently encountered one of my students who took a class on the playwright August Wilson with me 15 years ago. She didn't become a poet. She didn't become a scholar. Instead, she's helping people on death row as a lawyer at the Equal Justice Initiative

(EJI). But she reminded me of things we studied together in that August Wilson seminar that help her do this work. She told me I said to her at one point, "Learning black literature is not just all about you." She said she brought that to her interview with EJI founder Bryan Stevenson, and he said that's exactly right. So she brings that idea from studying great black literature to her work, which is transforming her so much as she tries to be helpful in this broken justice system.

That's just to say that I think it's really neat that right now, in this generation of philanthropic leaders with a different set of experiences—life experience and professional experience—we bring some new tools to help people move through uncomfortable conversations and hopefully experience the real joy, I think, that comes with doing work that has a justice orientation.

DARREN: In terms of your own background, how were you inspired and brought to this work?

ELIZABETH: Even before my parents, my great-grandmother and great-grandfather helped found Tuskegee University with Booker T. Washington. To think that these people were born into slavery, and after the war they had this idea that all of these emancipated people needed an education, is very moving and inspiring to me.

The power of that idea—and the power of this realization that whatever your privileges are, you always have to share them with a larger community—is something that's just in my DNA and in my family through the generations. My grandmother was a social worker in Harlem; my grandfather worked in Harlem Hospital in the Harlem community. Again, they were this example of how you work in your community, and if you have the privilege of some education and you have the privilege of some skills, you're dead if those skills and privileges aren't shared.

What I've seen through all of these decades of teaching is—and the story I just told is one example—that it's very wonderful, first of all, to be with young people at that stage of life. It's also wonderful to see what they can do with new ideas about inclusion, as they realize not everybody is always in the room. Just because *you're* in the room doesn't mean that there aren't *other people* who deserve to be in the room with you—and you always have to bear that in mind as you move through life.

Finally, as an artist, as a poet, I think that, again, there's a mandate. You don't write it just to have written it; you write it to share it and to be surprised by humanity in different places, because you never know who a human being is or how you can touch them. This animates all of my work. The possibility of those circles expanding—and that's part of what I think philanthropy can do as well—is something that I believe in quite deeply.

DARREN: And as a poet, you're a rare bird in philanthropy.

ELIZABETH: Yes, I am. And being a poet and a scholar, both of those things require a very, very relentless attention to detail and to precision—to precision in language and communication and thinking—which is something that I hope I impart to the other people around me.

I also see and have always experienced how artists can be extraordinarily creative problem solvers. Artists are able to hold contradiction aloft. We can hold together more than one thing at the same time. Things don't always need to be neat and tidy.

Human beings are contradictory, so solutions take work and are intricate. An artist's practice is all about that. It's a very nice analog for thinking about how to solve complicated problems in philanthropy. So, I think we need to respect the voices of our creators, who very often are economically marginalized, but more important, are sometimes seen as the strange outsiders—because you never know where the solution will be. We need vision, and we need people who can see around corners. And we need to lift up those visions that can stir us and make us understand each other's humanity in ways that policy sometimes can't. I think that's the part of magic and the "secret sauce" I'm hoping my philanthropy will also be able to recognize, respect, and harness.

DARREN: Some people would think of the arts and humanities as this high-minded intellectual pursuit—as opposed to, say, death row and criminal justice reform. As a philanthropist, how do you think about this intersection between art and justice?

ELIZABETH: I think about Bryan Stevenson at EJI, and the extraordinary National Memorial for Peace and Justice that he has created. Bryan's work starts with lawyering and helping people, and with policy-making and law-affecting and law-changing. But there is a reason Bryan has created the justice juggernaut that he has: because he understands the power of storytelling. He understands the power of artful storytelling—that is what moves and stirs people and can actually make them change their minds because they have had a deeply human experience.

You could imagine if Bryan were just saving all these young people and going before the Supreme Court—that would be a great thing, and it would be valuable unto itself. But he has taken it to the next level, because he's spatialized it now with the Legacy Museum in a way that many, many more people will be able to understand the simple fact of an unjust society. And in his speaking and his widely read book *Just Mercy*, he uses storytelling to move people to justice.

I also think what's powerful about Bryan is that we don't just have an artistic rendering of this problem. Rather, we say to artists, "How do you interpret and see the problem and the solution?" We don't ask them to make a flag or make a poster. We say, "Give us your real vision."

You could not have told Sanford Biggers or Titus Kaphar or Hank Willis Thomas what image to make. It was Hank Willis Thomas's imagination that made that unforgettable piece for the Legacy Museum—all those hands up, arms coming up out of that concrete, in a way that if you've seen it, you will never forget it, and you will never forget how it makes you feel.

DARREN: Do you think that more philanthropy needs to be investing in those kinds of endeavors? In storytelling and narrative?

ELIZABETH: No, I think those of us who do it just need to do it brilliantly and with integrity. I actually don't think it is for everyone to do, because not everyone comes from a place of deep knowledge and expertise and commitment to the arts. I would rather see the Ford and Mellon foundations—and other places where history and staff and deep knowledge exist—do it really, really, really well.

I think the other thing that's interesting about money in the arts is that it doesn't always scale. You don't always need millions and millions of dollars to make an impact. Sometimes it costs a lot of money to make a thing, but sometimes it doesn't cost a lot of money to make a thing.

The poem I made for the EJI memorial cost exactly zero. It cost nothing. And hopefully, it will make people think. The sculptures, okay—it costs money to make them, and those artists were paid, which is appropriate. But when you think about the lasting value from that investment, it's pretty extraordinary and very economical.

DARREN: Right, but at the same time, there was an investment in you as an artist—in your creativity, or in Hank Willis Thomas's creativity. You got private scholarships from philanthropies; you got investments in human capital. One of my concerns is that in philanthropy, particularly newer philanthropy, there is all this movement around metrics: If you can't measure it, then it's not worth investing in, or it should not be a priority. It's like when [South African judge] Albie Sachs talks about how everyone deserves beauty. It appears that some philanthropists believe, yes, everyone deserves beauty, but beauty will have to come after . . . Well, fill in the blank for whatever their priority is.

ELIZABETH: Yes. This goes back to your question about metrics. This is where I feel excited, challenged—and actually I just talked with my Mellon arts colleagues to consider how we can really carefully say something about impact in the arts. Because I think there's this question like "Well, how do we measure it? We can't measure it" or else "What is the payoff? We're not seeing it. Show us what the payoff is."

Or, at the other end of the spectrum, which is probably where *I* came into philanthropy, the question is: "Measure it?

Why would we measure the value of art in the first place? Everybody knows that art moves the human soul in a unique way, and that it can't be measured."

And there's work on the arts and economic development in neighborhoods, and I think that's really useful, but it's only a piece of it. I cannot measure how many people—literally, and we would all agree with this, millions and millions of people understand that justice is not equal, just from having read *To Kill a Mockingbird* or even from having seen the movie. So, I think somewhere in between those two examples, I want to commit to doing some rigorous and useful thinking, and bring together other people in the field to push it forward.

DARREN: So, for organizations like the Ford Foundation and the Mellon Foundation that have been around a long time, what are the challenges for us, in terms of our work around justice?

ELIZABETH: Right now, I'm dissatisfied with the use of diversity language and thinking in philanthropy, because I think some of us have expressed that as a bottom-line value in how we do things: raising up marginalized voices. That characterized our work and my work at Ford, and that will continue to be an aspect of what I value across the board at Mellon.

But what we know also is that as the culture changes, some mainstream organizations that have been used to their centrality and to their funding sources feel they can't necessarily see themselves in some of these new definitions.

I don't look at that in a hostile and adversarial way. But as an organization, don't say, "Oh, now diversity is important, so I'm going to run over to these people and tell them to pay for the diversity that we should have been doing all along." I think that I'd rather let this be a moment where we look back to words that James Baldwin wrote a very long time ago, in the 1950s (and he was not being hostile): "This world is white no longer, and it will never be white again."[36]

And what he meant by that is this: Let's just look at the United States. This is a beautiful, complicated, multi-voiced, multi-experienced nation that actually holds together, even though sometimes it feels like those ties are very, very tenuous. But it is *one thing*. We are a community—a diverse community. That is a fact. There is richness and beauty and power there.

And so, I think it's important for us to be partners in positive and rigorous thinking about how we learn from each other, and to ask, how is that a value of philanthropy? How can we help encourage communities where many voices at their best levels can be at the table?

I think that stage one, the challenge for me, is talking about why these spaces, why these values, why these tools matter in the culture at large. There is going to be some dissenting: "Why do we need arts and culture? Why do we need the humanities?" These things are under serious assault. So, I think talking about a renaissance and those values—talking about the importance of preserving things and making them precious so they're not lost in digitization—is stage one.

But a very quick stage two is this: If these valuable things are accessible to some, we have to make them accessible to all.

When I talked about this idea in the interview process with my board, I said, "That is the justice vision that I think is inherent in the work Mellon does. And I want to know that you all are comfortable with my articulating that, because that's how I see it."

And one of my board members—and I thought this was wonderful—said, "We think of ourselves as doing the right thing."

And I thought, *You have that kind of wonderful, old-fashioned value of doing the right thing.* And you know what? We know what that is. That's another way of saying justice.

3

THE AWARENESS OF IGNORANCE

LEARNING WHAT WE DON'T KNOW

It is certain, in any case, that ignorance, allied with power, is the most ferocious enemy justice can have.[37]

—James Baldwin

I recently found myself sitting inside the gates of the San Quentin State Prison in California with the legendary arts patron and philanthropist Agnes Gund, known to her family and friends as "Aggie."

Aggie is an 80-year-old grandmother; a graduate of Miss Porter's School, Connecticut College, and Harvard University; and president emerita of the Museum of Modern Art in New York. She's more likely to be seen on Park Avenue than walking past the gates and guards and metal detectors of a men's prison. So, you might be wondering, as her friends certainly did: What was Aggie doing there?

The answer: Aggie was there to learn.

Months before this visit, the idea of Agnes Gund in a prison might have been unfathomable. But after watching Ava DuVernay's powerful documentary *13th*—which tackles the connection between slavery and mass incarceration in the United States— Aggie was stunned. She left the theater and later said, "I went home and decided that this is what I had to do."[38]

She called me the day after seeing the film, looking for advice. And not just me. She started talking with experts, continued her education, met with DuVernay in her home, read Michelle Alexander's seminal 2010 book *The New Jim Crow*— all to replace what had been ignorance of the problem with information about it.

Horrified by the state of the justice system, the statistics about mass incarceration, and the implications for her own grandchildren (six of whom are black), Aggie chose to direct her philanthropy toward justice. In 2017, she sold one of her prized works of art—a Roy Lichtenstein painting titled *Masterpiece*—and used some of the proceeds to start the Art for Justice Fund, which will invest more than $100 million toward criminal justice reform. At a moment when philanthropy was often overlooking criminal justice reform, and when patrons of the arts like Aggie were more likely to be simply generous in their philanthropy rather than actively just, Aggie created a platform for others to contribute to systemic change.

Given her work in this field, and her newfound knowledge of the problem, Aggie did not need to visit a prison. She had done her homework and had done good work. Yet even after the fund was launched, the criminal justice system was something that Aggie had limited experience with. So, recognizing that she did not know the realities faced by incarcerated people, she decided to see that reality for herself.

That day at San Quentin, our guide was a man whose life could not have been more different from hers. He was black, had been convicted at age 16, and was now serving a sentence of 35 years to life. His beard had grayed since he'd been in jail. As they talked—Aggie in a stylish but practical down vest; her tour guide in a jacket labeled "Prisoner"—I felt sadness, but also hope. These two people, with such vastly different lives, were standing shoulder to shoulder, walking hand in hand, committed to the same arc of justice.

Aggie understood that it's not enough to have goodwill or to want to fix the problem. You need to figure out what you don't know—and identify areas where you may have, unbeknownst to you, biases or prejudices that stand in the way of doing justice. And if you are going to genuinely and meaningfully effect change, you need to get beyond your comfort zone.

By leaving her comfortable apartment, seeing firsthand what prison life was like, and speaking directly with the people she wished to help, Aggie moved beyond generosity to justice. And in our current sociopolitical climate, especially in the United States, that might be the model for all of us: to start by confronting our ignorance and our limitations, and ask what we can do to help, and then hold our hands open for others to lead the way.

In August 2017, many watched in horror as white supremacists marched in the streets of Charlottesville, emboldened by the ignorant and racist statements of those in power. Images of people brandishing Nazi and Confederate flags, and videos capturing offensive, racist, anti-semetic chants, were seen and heard across the country and the world. It was a disturbing portrait of the ignorance present in our world today.

Too often, we are confronted by displays of ignorance like these that are as obvious as they are abhorrent, and we recognize them immediately. The symbols and slurs used to target people based on their race, ethnicity, religion, or sexual orientation are well known, frowned upon, and fought against. We know how important it is to stand up against the most blatant forms of ignorance and bias, to confront racism and prejudice wherever we see it.

But it's also important to note that when we think about ignorance and bias, we are inclined to picture people and systems extremely different from those we find comfortable and familiar. We are tempted to focus on the most extreme instances.

The truth is, to see what ignorance and bias look like, we need only look in a mirror. For every instance of blatant ignorance and bias—of, for example, extreme prejudice and racism—there are subtler ways that these forces infect our own thinking and impede the work of social justice.

Unfortunately, and often unintentionally, ignorance is baked into the way we see the world, an ingredient inherent in our assumptions and attitudes. And even though some of the extreme examples of discrimination from our history that we remember and reference—like legalized segregation—have been defeated in the United States and other countries, subtler forms of discrimination and manifestations of bias are still present all around us.

These less visible forms of bias have real impacts on individuals, organizations, and communities alike. Researchers reported in *Harvard Business Review* that after performing a meta-analysis of 90 different studies on discrimination and its consequences, they found "across every job and individual outcome, the effects of subtle discrimination were at least as bad as, if not worse than, overt discrimination."[39] According to this research, that's because subtle bias happens more often—and when it does, we spend more time and energy trying to figure out what happened, and have little to no recourse to resolve the situation.

What's more, when "allied with power," as acclaimed writer (and Ford Foundation grantee) James Baldwin put it, our ingrained ignorance results in the neglect of certain people or issues that do not affect us directly, or in the preferential treatment of people and programs that conform to our existing biases or beliefs.

So, in the same ways that we might be unaware of our privileges, we might be equally unaware of our ignorance. David Rockefeller Jr. explained it well: "I think that I, along with most people, am not even aware of my knee-jerk racist, classist, and generally negative views. And I think it takes a lot of work to become aware enough that you see your own biases. I, like everybody, have work to do."

David is right. We all have work to do.

As leaders, we must ask ourselves: *What do we* not *know about? What biases do we bring to the table? What ignorance do we harbor? And whom must we talk to, where must we go, and what must we do to learn more about the areas and experiences where we may lack expertise?*

Often the trouble is that we do not know what we do not know. And as a result of inequality and the compounding influence of biases over time, we may find ourselves surrounded by people who share certain biases—our bubble—rather than those who can keep our ignorance in check and expand our perspective. Indeed, the pervasive power of ignorance is so terrible *because* it grips even the best-intentioned actors.

I know this because I experienced it myself.

Early in my tenure as president of the Ford Foundation, we took a hard look at our culture, our assets, and our programming, and sought to determine how we could have a more transformational impact. To do that, we worked hard on improving the organizational culture. We invested in an update of our building in New York, and we reimagined how we use some of our other assets, like our endowment, to support justice. The largest piece, of course, was reorienting all of our programming to address inequality in all of its forms.

Articulating and defining Ford*Forward*, and redirecting our work toward the issue of inequality, was a months-long process, and included hours of conversations and input from hundreds of people inside and outside the foundation. But when we announced Ford*Forward* to the world, something unexpected happened.

Jennifer Laszlo Mizrahi, the president of RespectAbility—one of our most valued and constructive partners—wrote me a rather scorching email calling me a hypocrite. And I deserved it.

To my deep regret, my grand articulation of our strategy going forward had made no mention of a huge community: the one billion people around the world who live with some form of disability, 80 percent of them in developing countries.[40]

Jennifer was just one of many with the same message, from former governor Tom Ridge and Carol Glazer—the chairman and president, respectively, of the National Organization on Disability—to my friend Micki Edelsohn, the co-founder of a remarkable organization called the Homes for Life Foundation in Wilmington, Delaware. Micki wrote to me, "I applaud you for taking on inequality. But when you talk about inequality, how can you not acknowledge people with disabilities?"

People with disabilities—both visible and invisible—face harsh inequalities that are relevant to every area in which we work. According to the US Census Bureau and the US Department of Labor, the poverty rate among people with disabilities is more than double that of people without disabilities.[41] People with disabilities are half as likely to be employed[42] or have a bachelor's degree.[43]

Many others reiterated Micki's message, and each time I got this type of feedback, my heart sank deeper into my stomach. I was shocked. How had we had missed this? I was embarrassed by my own ignorance. I was humbled—and a little horrified—by my own bias. Somehow, the checks and balances that I thought were built into our institution had failed to catch one of the most persistent and pervasive forms of injustice in the world.

I am a leader in a privileged sector. I didn't attend private schools or come from wealth, and I am conscious of the ways classist biases might manifest. As a black and gay man, I've witnessed many forms of ignorance in my own life, forms that demonstrate varying degrees of intentionality or aggression. Before this experience, I would have thought that I'd be able to spot even inadvertent discrimination, or that one of the many people working on this strategy would have raised the issue— but I could not remember a single time I had raised the issue in all those months.

I kept asking myself: *How could I have overlooked this critical dimension of inequality? How could our entire organization have overlooked it?*

Well, those who courageously—and correctly—raised this complicated set of issues had the answer. They pointed out that the Ford Foundation did not have a person with visible disabilities on our leadership team; did not make any affirmative effort to hire people with disabilities; did not consider people with disabilities in our strategy; and did not even provide those with physical disabilities with adequate access to our website, events, social media, or building. Our nearly 50-year-old headquarters was only minimally accessible to those with physical disabilities. It should go without saying: All of this was at odds with our mission.

Made aware of our ignorance, we knew we had to make meaningful change as an organization. The first and most important step was acknowledging our own fallibility and seeking out counsel from people who knew more than we did. After speaking with countless disability rights advocates and people with disabilities, we began to incorporate and include disability considerations into all the work we did at the Ford Foundation. We trained program officers, had difficult conversations, and brought experts onto our staff. We started taking practical action to address our hiring practices, and we revised our plan to renovate our headquarters to ensure it was physically accessible and welcoming to all people.

Thanks to this systematic and intentional approach, we made over $5 million in disability-specific grants in 2017 and 2018. Through these grants, and through other efforts we've made within the foundation, we have produced real impact and even become a leader in the disability justice space in a relatively short amount of time—all because we made our existing programming more inclusive for people with disabilities.

I learned so much from this experience. But first and foremost, I learned that to truly fight for justice, we must put pride aside, acknowledge our deficiencies, and call on people who will help us understand every side of every issue.

When I'm in a room, I always ask myself: Who can't be in that room because they don't have my credentials or resources? What rooms does my privilege allow me to be in that others are not? What rooms has my privilege historically kept people out of? And then, if I'm in the room, what am I going to do with it? Am I going to own who I am and be unapologetic about it? How do I confront ignorance without getting in someone's face—and make sure they don't forget what they've learned?

—MELLODY HOBSON, PRESIDENT OF ARIEL INVESTMENTS

Confronting your ignorance, uncovering your biases, and learning more is not something you accomplish. Rather, it is an ongoing process, one you have to engage in time and again. For different organizations and individuals, at different moments, this process takes different forms.

In 2017, I went to London to see an exhibit the Ford Foundation had supported: *Soul of a Nation: Art in the Age of Black Power*. This collection of pieces captured a short but powerful period in America's history—1963 to 1983—and taught its viewers about how conversations on civil rights and Black Power manifested themselves in the works of African American artists. Walking through the exhibit, I was deeply moved.

And yet it was hard to forget that the people most affected by the ideas and issues depicted in these works—the very Americans this exhibit was meant to inspire—were the least likely to see it.

If they wanted to take in the art made by their forebears, they would have to cross an ocean to visit one of the most expensive cities in the world.

The philanthropist and arts patron Alice Walton immediately recognized this problem and leapt at the chance to fix it. She found the exhibit a home at the Crystal Bridges Museum of American Art, where it ran for several months in 2018, and in doing so presented this powerful examination of the US civil rights movement in a place where communities directly connected to and affected by these events could connect through art.

This is part of the project—and the philosophy—behind Crystal Bridges. This oasis of art and culture opened its doors in 2011,[44] and ever since then Alice has made a concerted effort to bring in art that is powerful and relevant to the Arkansas community.

The idea behind the museum is simple: "When people go through the galleries," Alice told me, "they should see themselves on the walls and relate to our melting-pot country." So instead of filling the museum with art purely from her own perspective, she makes sure to acknowledge her own bias, and works to select art that would appeal to a wider audience.

Of course, acknowledging one bias is not always enough. Often, multiple predispositions and prejudices can come into play. That was the case for Alice and her team in the early days of Crystal Bridges:

When we first opened the museum, my total focus was on just setting it up and getting it running. Then we started looking at our own internal research: who our visitors were, how often they came, whom they brought with them—those kinds of metrics. And we were shocked and dismayed to discover that while we were getting an economically diverse set of visitors (likely because the museum's galleries are free), we were not getting an ethnically diverse set of visitors. Simply put, the makeup of our visitors did not reflect the diverse community we were operating in.

Alice and her team were puzzled. Their art collection, while not as diverse as they wanted it to be, was much more ethnically and racially diverse than in most museums. So why did the museum's visitors not match its art?

When the team turned that reflection inward, they realized the problem was *them*. The people running the museum and working at it did not reflect the community they were trying to serve. This whole time, they thought they knew what was best to get a more diverse audience, when really, they needed a more diverse internal staff to help guide them.

After acknowledging this need, Alice and her team took action. "We changed our hiring policies," she said. "From then on, before we hired someone, we made sure our hiring pool was diverse, and that little tweak made a world of difference. Soon our staff diversified—and along with it, our audience diversified too." Alice is proud to say that now, in terms of visitors, the museum probably has more diversity than the community itself.

Seeing this kind of change on the level of one museum made Alice more conscious of the way this dynamic operates at all museums. I feel so fortunate that my Ford Foundation colleagues and I have been able to partner with Alice and the Walton Family Foundation on the Diversifying Art Museum Leadership Initiative, to make sure more people and more communities are represented in the world of art. Together, we have committed $6 million to support 20 programs for museums across the country as they develop initiatives to nurture talent and diversify their curatorial and management staff.

At all of these institutions, we are trying to implement what Alice learned. As she put it, in order to ensure your museum or institution "reflects the diversity of the community," you have to "take an active role, get out of the institution, and go into the community." And that's not just true for museums: All of us can think about diversifying our hiring and leadership to expand our perspectives and prevent our institutions from incubating ignorance or enacting bias.

No matter your position or perspective—and regardless of your organization or orientation—identifying your ignorance and weeding out latent biases are crucial steps in the march toward justice. That may mean bringing diverse perspectives into your organization . . . or taking responsibility for your ignorance . . . or leaving your own comfort zone, and going to places and spaces that challenge you to see the world differently. Because until we rid ourselves of our prejudices, both conscious and unconscious, we risk leaving people behind.

JOYFUL JUSTICE

A Conversation with Laurene Powell Jobs

Wherever Laurene Powell Jobs goes, she arrives armed with a list—not of what she wants to talk about, but of whom. These are the names of people doing what she calls "God's work": people on the ground, and the organizations working with them, who inspire her with their fights against injustice.

Laurene's list includes well-known activists like Bryan Stevenson, leaders like Elisa Villanueva Beard and Bill Bynum, and artists like JR and Anna Deavere Smith. Many others are people working quietly behind the scenes: Andrew Youn, the co-founder and executive director of the One Acre Fund. Ali Noorani from the National Immigration Forum. David Domenici, who runs the Center for Educational Excellence in Alternative Settings. Christa Gannon, who started an organization that works with kids in the juvenile justice system. The list goes on and on.

That is Laurene's way. Instead of shining a light on herself, she shines it on others.

Years ago, people may have identified Laurene through her late husband, Steve Jobs. But today, people know her as a pioneering activist and philanthropist, forging her own unique path toward a more just world. In 2004, Laurene was one of the first to try an increasingly popular model for newer philanthropists, by forming a limited liability corporation called Emerson Collective. Since then, she has used the organization and every tool at her disposal to challenge the systems that create inequality.

Laurene supports movements from the bottom up, lobbies leaders from the top down, and engages in politics and philanthropy side by side. She also gets behind people she believes in and brings together partners from all kinds of fields. Working together, they dedicate their time, energy, and resources to some of the world's biggest issues: from education and immigration reform to the need for strong independent journalism and social justice leadership.

DARREN: You have supported a lot of racial justice work. You've supported investing in a lot of people-of-color-led organizations and specific entrepreneurs. From a philanthropist's perspective, what does justice look like for you?

LAURENE: Actually, justice in philanthropy looks like philanthropy to me—I don't separate the two.

To explain what I mean, we have to back up to how I first became involved in the social sector, because I'm an accidental social justice activist.

I was invited, when I was perhaps 29 years old, to speak to a class of seniors at a local high school. Their teacher asked me to talk about college, education, and my experiences—she often tried to have guests come on Fridays.

It was the first time that I had ever been in a high school in California, because I didn't grow up there. I had a notion that the education system in California was excellent, a model that other schools followed. And that was indeed true back in the '70s.

But in 1978, when Proposition 13 went through, it changed the equation for how often property taxes are assessed, which had the effect of flattening funding for public schools. The "smoothing formula" the state gave to low-income communities was totally insufficient—so by the time I was in that classroom at Carlmont High School in 1994, they hadn't had any escalation in funding for 13 years.

So, the school I walked into was one where there were literally broken windows. There were doors off hinges. There were kids in massive parkas and 4XL pants, and I had this sense that these kids were so frightened they had to make themselves larger, as one does when one encounters a bear in the woods. You want to claim more space than you have. That's what was going through my mind.

When I went into the class and sat with the students, they were so sweet and gentle and open and curious, just like high school students are everywhere. They were full of promise and questions. I started talking to them, but then I told them, "Just ask me questions." And it was unconventional for them because usually they just sat there and listened.

And they started asking me, "What is college like?" and "What kind of classes did you get?"

I responded with a question of my own: "How many of you have been on a college campus?"

Maybe one or two.

"How many of you have siblings who are in college?"

Again, maybe one or two.

Eventually I asked, "How many of you have taken the SAT?"

None.

So I asked the teacher, "Who's advising all of these amazing students?"

And she said, "Well, this high school of 1,600 full-time students has one advisor in a small office, and one part-time person who writes to colleges and collects pamphlets, but the answer is, basically, no one. Nobody has stepped up."

So, I said to them, "Okay, I'm going to be your college counselor for the next month. I'm coming back every Friday, and I'm going to work with each of you."

DARREN: So, you came back on Fridays to be their counselor?

LAURENE: Yes, for the next 12 weeks. And I learned that, of the 35 students, only three had the classes that they needed to apply to a four-year college.

DARREN: And that was a turning point for you?

LAURENE: Yes. At the time I was running a natural foods company. I had 50 people working for me. But I'm still angry about it. I'm still horrified. I'm still offended. When you see injustice like that, in person, you don't stay the same. They lacked one year of English, or one year of math, or a life science or a foreign language, and nobody told them they needed it. I was the first one to tell them all of these things.

DARREN: It sounds like rather than getting sad, you got enraged.

LAURENE: I was so many things. I was enraged. I was affected. I was, in a way, ashamed that a public education that had served me so well, that was truly my portal to opportunity—an education that I held dear and that I believed was a core value of America and a necessary structure for a well-functioning democracy—was not being delivered to students in an equal and just way. This experience made that absolutely, abundantly clear.

That insight became the cornerstone of my work for the rest of my life.

DARREN: Has that informed how you created Emerson Collective?

LAURENE: Absolutely. To this day, Emerson works with students and their families. So, yes, that informed the creation of Emerson, as well as all of our deep work in education, including the creation of the XQ Institute, the philanthropic portfolio, our ed tech investment portfolio, and our whole body of work around immigration reform. That started in 2001, with the DREAM Act advocacy for our first class of graduating high school students, many of whom were undocumented and couldn't access state or federal funding for their education.

DARREN: So, you had firsthand experience with Dreamers?

LAURENE: Correct—for 16 years. And I made my first trip to Washington, D.C., as an advocate around the Dream Act. I called then Senator Jon Corzine, who was my former boss, and he cosponsored the bill. I thought that we were going to pass the DREAM Act in 2001, or 2003, or 2007. Then I thought it would be in 2008, or 2013, or 2014.

DARREN: But it also sounds like your philanthropy is very much fused with the political realities of activism too.

LAURENE: If you pull one thread, it's connected to the whole fabric. And you can't just keep pulling one thread. You actually have to put your hand on the fabric. Then you'll realize: "We need to reweave this."

DARREN: And that really does require both a philanthropic investment and an investment in the political process?

LAURENE: It does.

DARREN: For a lot of people, that second part—the political part—is the part they don't like. A lot of philanthropists aren't really comfortable in that space.

LAURENE: Except justice is political! You need courage not only in civil society, but in governance. You need courage from all of your elected officials and leaders because everybody has a role to play. And without politics and policy change, you're not going to get the change that you need at scale.

DARREN: How did you come to see issues of race and gender in all of this? Because a lot of your work has focused on issues of racial inequity, like with the Dreamers, or the issues that Bryan Stevenson is dealing with, like the legacy of slavery.

LAURENE: It's simple. Resources are unequally distributed across our country and across sectors. So, you have to look at where it's being unfairly distributed; it's often along lines of race and gender.

Education is a prime example, but you can really see this with any issue. You could look at environmental justice, as we do as well, and you could just see that in the more well-off communities that get the ear of the politicians, a lot of environmental problems are solved, and a lot of the systems still work. You don't see lead in the water in Palo Alto, but you see it across the country in low-income communities of color.

In fact, low-income communities are at the nexus of great inequities in every single system that they touch. Those coming into the world who are needing the most, those who are the most impoverished and the most imperiled, end up receiving the least. That's backwards. The systems need to be redesigned so that those who need the most receive the most. Those who need the most in educational resources need to receive the most in educational resources.

DARREN: You see things clearly through a lens of systems analysis, which sets you apart. Some people say, "I can't take on the system. I want to focus on one school," or "I want to focus on one family."

LAURENE: This is my full-time work. I think for a lot of people who think that way, it's impossible for them to take on the system unless they are devoting all their time, energy, and resources to an issue. And then, if you're doing that, you won't be satisfied in just helping one school, because you can't unsee what you've seen.

So, when you understand the scale and scope of inequity, most people will feel like if they *can* respond, they *must* respond. That only happens, though, if you're deep in it. And that requires a full-time investment.

For me, this is the most joyful, happy-making work on the planet. We get to think all day long about how to redesign unjust systems. How great is that? And we get to work with people who are doing something about injustice and inequity.

DARREN: It's interesting that you use the word "joy." What brings you joy as a philanthropist?

LAURENE: I think it's the highest privilege in life to be a part of positive change in a person's life. It's important to understand that you can improve the life of another through your own efforts. And that that is the highest purpose of humanity.

For me to be, in some way, that inflection point in a young person's life, or to be associated with people or organizations that are that inflection point in someone's life—it's happy-making. It fills my soul. It fills my spirit. It causes me to get up excited, every single day, to see what we can get accomplished.

4

THE OWNERSHIP
OF SELFLESSNESS

GIVING WITH HUMILITY

*The most truly generous persons are those who give silently
without hope of praise or reward.*[45]

—*Carol Ryrie Brink*

In many circles, Chuck Feeney is known as the "James Bond of
philanthropy."[46] After earning a great fortune in the duty-free
shopping business, Chuck has spent more than 30 years pursuing
his own secret mission: to go broke.

He's well on his way to fulfilling his desire. To date, Chuck
has given away over $8 billion.[47] And he has been able to do it, for
the most part, in absolute secrecy.

Determined to keep his philanthropic endeavors hidden,
and directly inspired by Carnegie's "The Gospel of Wealth," in
1984 Chuck funneled all of his assets into a foundation he named
The Atlantic Philanthropies.[48] Since then, the foundation has

supported higher education, public health, human rights campaigns, and scientific research. It helped provide access to AIDS treatments in southern Africa and offered the necessary financial support for a new public health system in Vietnam.[49]

Until Chuck went public with his story in the wake of a 1997 lawsuit that threatened to blow his cover, the foundation operated in complete anonymity.[50] In the years since, Chuck has still maintained some measure of invisibility. To date, there is no building, program, or initiative that bears his name—and he refuses to have it any other way.

As Dr. David Skorton told me, for years Chuck has said the same thing over and over: "I want my last check to bounce." After the two worked together on a number of projects for Cornell University, Chuck's alma mater, David wanted to use the Feeney name "to inspire future generations of philanthropists."[51] Knowing Chuck would be fiercely opposed to the idea of naming a building or hall in his honor, David settled on something that might inspire others to follow in Chuck's footsteps. "I told him I'd like to set up a national award, a medal in philanthropy named for him."

Chuck swiftly vetoed it.

"'I told you I'm not going to do this. Now stop asking!'" Skorton recalled Chuck saying. "It was hilarious."

As we work to reimagine Carnegie's gospel for the twenty-first century—and move from generosity toward justice—Chuck's story should inspire each of us to ask a critical question: *Are we more concerned about others' liberation or our legacy?*

In philanthropy, there is a long-established tradition of rewarding generous donors with a naming ceremony. Buildings are named in benefactors' honor in exchange for large monetary contributions. The pomp and circumstance that surround these dedication events not only draw attention to the contributions, but guarantee the contributors' names will live on long after their death.

We all hope those people we know well, and even those we don't, will remember the best of us: our presence, our accomplishments, our life. This is a desire we all share, regardless of our level of wealth or prestige. But those of us engaged in philanthropy must be especially careful not to conflate this desire to build legacy with our responsibility to do good. If we're not cautious of this ego-driven aspiration, we're at risk of giving back in ways that service vanity more than justice.

Sometimes naming opportunities can distort our incentives and drive donations toward some causes and not others. To George Kaiser, chairman and majority owner of BOK Financial Corporation and founder of the George Kaiser Family Foundation, this causes an obvious problem:

> *Naming opportunities are usually attached to physical structures, not programs. It's wonderful to have a ballet, opera, or philharmonic. It's wonderful to have libraries. But these are institutions predominantly patronized by the wealthy. You rarely see naming opportunities attached to, say, programs in early childhood education. The compelling moral purpose, rather than the recognition, should drive the gift.*

Having amassed his wealth from oil and gas, commercial banking, and private equity, George has pledged to donate his remaining net worth to the foundation. Deeply aware of the advantages he gained as a child by having caring parents, a good education, and the freedom that comes with economic mobility,

George has focused his foundation on providing equal opportunities for young children. The foundation works to accomplish this mission by funding early childhood education, social service support, criminal justice assistance programs and advocacy, civic enhancement projects, and community health initiatives.

Most of the foundation's funding goes toward creating and operating programs intended to improve a young child's opportunity for mobility out of poverty. Those programs can show measurable success over time and are personally satisfying to the sponsor. But the foundation is also active in advocacy and policy work that may be even more important to those children—even if it's less emotionally satisfying for donors.

Too often, some of the most important forms of impact can't be seen or measured—and not being able to measure an outcome can kill a great program before it ever gets off the ground. John Arnold, co-chair of Arnold Ventures, argued that philanthropy tends to underfund policy work for that very reason:

> *Policy work is underinvested in because donors who contribute money for a capital campaign on a new building can point directly at the proverbial brick in the building and say, "I paid for this. And I can see directly the results of my contribution." With policy, it's difficult to know what the counterfactual would have been, or to try to understand success in the short and medium terms.*

John's assessment of current philanthropic attitudes is entirely correct. And it worries me, because pushing for new policies is some of the most important, most fundamental work philanthropists can do. At the Ford Foundation, we are proud of our legacy of supporting, for example, civil rights leaders like Nelson

Mandela, who sought to change the racist apartheid policies of his country. And the Ford Foundation, under the leadership of Frank Thomas, might never have given its support if it had required that Mandela provide quantitative proof of an outcome, or a bill or building the foundation could put its name on.

Jon Stryker took this idea a step further. A top stockholder in Stryker Corporation—a medical technology company founded by his grandfather, Dr. Homer Stryker[52]—Jon knows well the meaning of a name and the way legacy works. In 2000, he founded the Arcus Foundation, which is dedicated to LGBTQ social justice and great ape conservation. Originally, Arcus was going to be called the Jon Stryker Foundation. But then Jon realized something:

> *I didn't want it to be all about me. I wanted to build an institu-*
> *tion that symbolized something to people, that was a place people*
> *knew they could go to get assistance in their work. It was about a*
> *whole bunch of comrades working together. I was really trying to*
> *build a symbol of hope and intelligence and rationality. And Arcus*
> *has become that.*

Indeed, Jon's insight was that by taking his name off the foundation, he would help make the foundation less about him—and more about the causes he wanted to promote and the communities he hoped to build.

So, beyond questioning the intentionality behind our philanthropy, moving from generosity toward justice will also require us to ask ourselves another critical question: *Are we doing it because it's easy?* Having a building or university hall named in your honor offers almost instant gratification; it's tangible proof of your contribution. The immediate payoff can be deeply alluring, especially when your donation benefits a school, university, or church you attended. But in a time when inequality and injustice abound, that form of philanthropy—while very important—may not be the most valuable.

Acknowledging the ways we have been gifted with opportunities and resources unavailable to others is essential to the work of justice. It both allows us to see the systems of privilege at play and endows us with an ability to alter them for the betterment of all people. So, it's natural, after recognizing your privilege, to think you should support the institutions that gave you an advantage, to help others reach the same status.

There is no denying that the institutions we attend shape and mold us in significant ways. But when it comes to giving back, it is always worth asking the question: *Where are my resources most needed?*

Although donating to educational institutions and religious organizations is commendable, institutions and programs that are already well resourced and well funded may not need our contributions the most. Though these entities do good work, justice may be better served if we invest in places and programs that are underfunded and lacking resources. The emotional payoff of these investments may not be as immediate or tangible, but they are far more profitable to the cause of justice.

In the end, addressing these dichotomies in philanthropy—legacy versus justice, doing what is easy versus doing what is hard—ultimately comes down to one thing: ego. And unfortunately, even after we have acknowledged our privilege, even after we have confronted bias, even after we have chosen to actively pursue justice, ego can still get in our way.

One of the problems facing philanthropy is that so much of it is based on the life experiences of the philanthropists themselves. Probably 60 percent of American philanthropy is dedicated to colleges and universities, religious institutions, health care facilities, medical research, and naming opportunities related to those causes. These are all institutions that have been important in the lives of philanthropists, and they do a lot of good, but they're not necessarily the most effective or morally compelling targets for philanthropy to focus on.

—GEORGE KAISER, FOUNDER OF THE GEORGE KAISER
FAMILY FOUNDATION

Practicing a New Gospel of Wealth doesn't necessitate the death of our ego, but it does require us to monitor it. To effectively move away from generosity and toward justice, we must learn to decenter our personal aspirations and agendas. Although we may find ourselves in positions of leadership in philanthropy, it's not all about us. "It is leadership not solely for the advancement of one's self, but intentionally for the advancement of others," as Laura Arrillaga-Andreessen rightly pointed out in the definition of her new leadership archetype: "legacy leadership."

Ego does not affect only individuals and leaders in philanthropy. The temptation is present also for institutions to demonstrate how their contributions deliver impact, a tendency that inevitably stifles collaborations that would make credit harder to assign. When we seek credit over collaboration—even with the best intentions or to justify our continued investment—we can let egos and logos get in the way of impact. This limits the ways we can work together toward justice.

If anyone appreciates the effectiveness of philanthropy from a place of humility, it's Strive Masiyiwa. In 1993, Strive founded Econet Group in his home country of Zimbabwe.[53] After overcoming a legal battle with the state to receive a license, he grew the company into a multinational telecommunications group across 29 countries and became Zimbabwe's first billionaire.[54]

Almost from the beginning (since 1996), Strive and his wife, Tsitsi, founded and built Higherlife Foundation, an organization dedicated to providing access to high-quality education for 250,000 young African students over the past 20 years.[55] And beyond his personal philanthropy, Strive is also a luminary in the philanthropic sector, having served for over 15 years on the board of trustees of The Rockefeller Foundation.[56] Despite having such an inspiring story and impressive résumé, Strive reminds us, "Philanthropy is at its best when you do something and you don't need credit."

As individuals and organizations with vast amounts of wealth and resources, we are at an increased risk of self-aggrandizement. Rather than seeing those affected by systems of oppression and injustice as co-laborers with us, we can begin to see ourselves as "saviors." It is a powerful mindset that tempts even the best among us.

Remember Dr. Martin Luther King Jr.'s conviction that while "philanthropy is commendable," we must not "overlook the circumstances of economic injustice which make philanthropy necessary."[57] No doubt, King's leadership and legacy should inspire all philanthropists, activists, and lovers of justice. In fact, I'm sure that when any of us think of visionary leaders who have inspired large groups of people to join the fight for social justice, King is at the top of our list. And yet, as awe-inspiring and revolutionary as he was, he too was not immune to the pitfalls of the human ego.

While many people instantly associate the civil rights movement with King, a lesser-known but no less important leader in the movement was Ella Baker. Born in Norfolk, Virginia, Baker was committed to the cause of justice from a young age.[58] As a small child, she heard her grandmother's tales of slave life. By the time she joined the Young Negroes' Cooperative League—an organization created to foster black economic power through collective action—in 1930, Baker had internalized the importance of fighting for the marginalized. That unwavering conviction led her to Atlanta in 1957, where she helped run King's Southern Christian Leadership Conference and, later, the Student Nonviolent Coordinating Committee.[59]

Even though Baker worked closely with King and his organization, she did not hesitate to draw attention to issues she felt hindered their effectiveness, even when they involved King himself. In addition to deriding the sexism that pervaded the Southern Christian Leadership Conference's patriarchal structure, she also critiqued the towering, larger-than-life persona associated with King. In her book, *Ella Baker and the Black Freedom Movement*, Professor Barbara Ransby argues that "Baker felt the focus on King drained the masses of confidence in themselves. People often marveled at things King could do that they could not; his eloquent speeches overwhelmed as well as inspired."[60] Unafraid to share her dissenting thoughts with King directly, Baker asked him, at one point, why he allowed people to view him in such a grandiose, hero-like way. King replied that it was simply what people wanted.[61]

While there is no doubting King's leadership, Baker's criticism of King was valid. The "savior" persona that surrounded King—a persona he didn't explicitly push back against—helped galvanize followers, but sometimes distracted from the movement. Rather than focusing on the collective grassroots efforts of individuals from all backgrounds, often the attention was unduly devoted to King.

Just consider the way we perceive the civil rights movement today. Growing up, every child learns Martin Luther King Jr.'s name. Schools and streets are named after him. He has his own holiday. But why is the same not true for all the other on-the-ground organizers in the movement—particularly for the women and LGBTQ people laboring in King's shadow? Critical figures like Diane Nash, Septima Clark, Bayard Rustin, Dorothy Height, and Fannie Lou Hamer are too often ignored—and that's partially because King's towering public persona was allowed to eclipse their efforts.

Now we can only wonder: What would it have meant for the civil rights movement—for young women and LGBTQ people back then, and even today—if these powerful role models had seen more time in the spotlight? What could it have meant, for people around the world, if their examples had been used to remind us of the personal power we all have, as individuals, to create change? Unfortunately, we will never know.

Doing justice is not easy work. It can be hard, tedious, and unrelenting. Tearing down the oppressive institutions that have denied individuals opportunities and freedoms for far too long requires much from us—including deep humility. And even the best of us, including Dr. Martin Luther King Jr., can fall short of that requirement at times.

Whenever I consider the importance of humility, I remind myself that this fight is bigger than all of us. Conversely, the same holds true for whenever I feel the symptoms of imposter syndrome and begin to doubt my own abilities. I remember that no one has to do this alone and, more important, no one has all the answers.

Accepting this truth may come with discomfort. After all, no one wants to feel inadequate or insufficient. But in this moment, I believe we are being called to lean into this uneasiness. As Laura Arrillaga-Andreessen put it, we're being summoned to "find comfort in discomfort."

We will not always get it right. We will make mistakes. We will need help. We will fall short—even the best among us do from time to time. But we can take proactive steps to ensure we are always decentering ourselves and centering the cause of justice. We can check our privilege, confront our own biases, temper our egos, and exercise humility. When we take these precautionary measures with earnest conviction, we are well on the path toward doing justice. In fact, it means we're ready for the next step: seeking out the root causes of *in*justice.

5

THE RAISING OF ROOTS

ADDRESSING CAUSES, NOT CONSEQUENCES

The opposite of poverty is not wealth; the opposite of poverty is justice.[62]
—Bryan Stevenson

When we think of images that illustrate justice, a supermarket may not be the first thing that comes to mind. And yet when Pathmark opened on 125th Street in Harlem in 1999, local residents were finally given something they had deserved for 30 years: a well-stocked supermarket.[63]

Prior to Pathmark's arrival, supermarket chains had avoided Harlem. Concerned about shoplifting and the community's supposed lack of buying power, stores stayed away. But after having success in other inner-city areas, Pathmark decided to give this historic New York neighborhood a try.

The Pathmark supermarket was built by the Abyssinian Development Corporation, a Harlem-based nonprofit organization I had the honor of serving back in 1994. Dedicated to revitalizing the community, ADC has worked to develop a wide range of projects, all with the goal of empowering residents to be masters of their own social, cultural, and economic lives. Rather than simply addressing the community's lack of access to fresh foods or its housing problem, ADC has been addressing a root cause of these issues: a lack of investment in the neighborhood.

When we look out at the world, we can identify many unjust outcomes that merit our attention and concern. Millions are unsure about where their next meal is coming from. Many families, both here and abroad, are struggling to find affordable housing, or indeed any housing at all. Natural disasters devastate entire communities—particularly poorer communities—around the world. As individuals involved in philanthropy, we may respond to these troubling realities by funding world hunger initiatives or opening homeless shelters, or contributing to relief and rebuilding projects. While these efforts are commendable and help solve immediate needs, they do not necessarily address the systemic issues that produced the problems.

This is partly because the symptoms of our biggest problems often are highly visible. The urgent distracts from the underlying. We see the individuals living on street corners. We hear about the children who are malnourished because there's no place to buy fresh fruits and vegetables in their neighborhood. We know of the many families struggling to buy basic school supplies for the new school year. Because we can so clearly observe these symptoms, addressing them is far easier than tackling the underlying diseases that caused them. Plus, it makes us more comfortable.

When we donate to a homeless shelter or sponsor a family for the holidays, it helps us alleviate the "survivor's guilt" we may have about our own privilege. It makes us feel good. But in the end, doing justice is not about doing what feels good; it's about *doing* good, and that goes far beyond charity.

Doing good means doing the uncomfortable work of exposing the reasons charity is necessary in the first place. That excavation process is not always pleasant. In fact, as I realized during my visit to the Equal Justice Initiative's National Memorial for Peace and Justice, it can be pretty painful.

When Bryan Stevenson founded EJI back in 1989, he wanted to help solve an immediate issue: the lack of legal representation for poor prisoners on death row in Alabama. Alabama prisoners who were unable to afford a lawyer had little to no options. There were no public defenders, and those appointed by the state got a maximum of $1,000 per case.[64] If you were wrongly convicted and on death row in Alabama, being poor was, literally, a death sentence.

EJI sought to change that.

As of 2016, EJI has helped over 115 people on death row reverse their sentences and, in some cases, gain their freedom.[65] And since its founding 30 years ago, it has expanded its legal aid capacity to include minors as well as people with physical and mental disabilities.[66]

In recent years, EJI has garnered national attention not only for its inspiring legal aid work but also for its unflinching commitment to unearthing the painful history that gave birth to America's mass incarceration crisis. Beyond addressing the visible injustices of the criminal justice system, EJI has been at the forefront of research on race, poverty, and the history of slavery and lynching in America. Similar to Michelle Alexander's work in *The New Jim Crow*, EJI research efforts are drawing direct connections between America's storied struggle with racism and white supremacy and the racial prejudice of its criminal justice system. What began as an organization with a simple mission—addressing one symptom of a diseased system—has become a leader in a larger movement to fight mass incarceration by addressing its underlying cause: racism.

EJI recognizes that solving the racial inequities of today will require the nation to grapple with its troubled past. It is keenly aware that there can be no true healing and restoration without an understanding that something is broken, and has been for a long time. So, beyond publishing research reports, EJI is facilitating this long-overdue reckoning process through its memorial.

On April 26, 2018, EJI's National Memorial for Peace and Justice in Montgomery, Alabama, opened to the public.[67] It is the nation's first memorial dedicated to "the legacy of enslaved black people, people terrorized by lynching, African Americans humiliated by racial segregation and Jim Crow, and people of color burdened with contemporary presumptions of guilt and police violence."[68] I had the honor of visiting this remarkable space on its opening day, and it was beyond moving. Walking through this memorial—reading the names of men, women, boys, and girls who were beaten, tortured, and lynched simply because of the color of their skin—was an immersion in pain, but it felt deeply necessary.

By creating the National Memorial for Peace and Justice, EJI has crafted a space where we, as a nation, can mourn the victims of injustice, reflect on the pain of inequality, and remember the horrors of the past. It has gifted us with an incredible opportunity to face the fundamental flaws of our history so we can better recognize their deep connection to our flawed present. Through both its research work and this memorial, EJI is illustrating what it means to go beyond the surface—to unearth the roots that nurture the fruits of injustice we see and so desperately desire to address.

I think one of the biggest challenges that we've had to overcome—and that we continue to work on—is that sometimes we focus too much on projects and too little on process. In fighting the most immediate problems, we sometimes gloss over the root causes. Because that is the matrix we have to work within: the resources that we receive are all for specific outcomes that we have to deliver. So we focus on those outcomes rather than the systemic issues.

—IKAL ANGELEI, FOUNDER OF FRIENDS OF LAKE TURKANA

Now, while it's one thing to make visible the root causes of inequality in our society, it's quite another to shift the systems that have grown as a result. We can't—and should not be tempted to—look only at the specifics of a case like Michael Brown or Eric Garner, or all the Michaels and Erics and Trayvons and Tamirs and Sandras we have lost. To understand what happened to them, and so many others like them, we have to look beyond the immediate. We have to grapple with the past and how it infects the present—how individual episodes are linked to larger social habits and forces. If we know that racism is at the root of mass incarceration, how do we fight the problem at the root? If we can trace wrongly convicted black defendants to discrimination in the court system, how do we confront bias on a structural level rather than just a personal one?

These are difficult questions, and there are no easy answers to uproot pervasive injustice. That said, when we start with root causes, innovative and just solutions can emerge. And not all of those solutions are going to come from programming. Just as seeking root causes reveals deeper structural issues, we might find solutions in reimagining our most fundamental systems and structures.

For example, take the recent work the Ford Foundation has been doing around impact investing and mission-related investments (MRIs).

Like all foundations, the Ford Foundation is a creature of capitalism. At one point in our early history, the foundation owned a majority of the nonvoting shares of the Ford Motor Company. The profits made from the selling of those shares in the mid-twentieth century, in addition to our current investments in the market, fund our endowment. As a major beneficiary of the free market economy, we benefit from a system that also creates inequities in our society.

Henry Ford II, the former president of the foundation, once wrote that we should "examine the question of our obligations to our economic system."[69] He challenged us to consider how the Ford Foundation, "as one of the [market] system's most prominent offspring, might act most wisely to strengthen and improve its progenitor."

To put it more bluntly, we were established by a market system and endowed by the money of the past century's 1 percent.

We are stewards of enormous resources—participants in and beneficiaries of a capitalist system. As a result, our work is quite literally enabled by returns on capital. In turn, I believe we are obligated "to strengthen and improve" the system to which we owe our good fortune.

My conviction is not anathema to capitalism. The great economist Adam Smith himself argued that the markets could not be blind to the condition of society, and that "no society can surely be flourishing and happy, of which the far greater part of the members are poor and miserable."[70] Smith was a visionary—not only the forefather of capitalism, but also the author of *The Theory of Moral Sentiments*, which he regarded as more important than his *The Wealth of Nations*. Philanthropy's role, he believed, is to contribute to the "flourishing" of the "far greater part"—to help foster a stronger safety net and a level playing field.

One step the Ford Foundation is taking to do this—to help correct the market's biggest weak point, inequality—is to rethink how we manage and utilize our endowment.

In 1969, US tax law mandated that foundations pay out a minimum of 6 percent of their total assets each year.[71] The percentage has since stabilized at 5 percent. For the Ford Foundation, in recent years, meeting this requirement has translated to an annual grant-making budget of around $600 million. Meanwhile, we put the other 95 percent of our assets to work in the investment market, with the goal of earning financial returns that sustain the grant-making power of our endowment over time.

In the spring of 2017, the foundation reimagined this standard protocol in philanthropy. After many months of analysis and planning, our Board of Trustees authorized the allocation of up to $1 billion of our endowment for mission-related investments (MRIs). These investments will allow us to achieve financial returns for our endowment while also addressing a root cause of injustice: a lack of investments in underserved communities.

In our market system, there is a deeply ingrained idea that we have to achieve the highest monetary returns; we value financial gains above all else. The by-product of this mentality is a kind of skepticism, or risk aversion, that tends to exacerbate inequality. Rather than investing in low-income areas, we are inclined to pool our investments in places that have already been "proven." And when it comes down to the types of investments we make, we don't always think of social returns as being as valuable as financial ones. If we cannot count or quantify the impact of our potential invest-ment, we shy away from that opportunity. As a result, we create an uneven market that is heavily funded in some areas and severely underfunded in others. It is no surprise that these neglected areas tend to be low-income communities and communities of color.

In many parts of the world, failing to invest in a commu-nity results in a lack of business activity in the area, which then results in a higher unemployment rate. And in most cases, a high unemployed rate is correlated with a high poverty rate, which leads to a whole host of issues: inability to afford healthy foods, lack of access to quality health care facilities, limited transpor-tation options, and understaffed public schools, just to name a few. This underlying investment problem—which often acts in tandem with other drivers of inequality—gives birth to an array of unjust outcomes.

Whether by choosing investments that make housing more affordable and inclusive, or by expanding access to vital financial services in low-income communities, MRIs will help us tackle this issue. By actively choosing to invest in "risky" areas where returns may not come as easily or in financial form, we are seeking to correct an underlying issue in the market. And by offering communities more affordable housing options and increasing their ability to secure loans and finance their businesses, MRIs will give these areas the kind of economic attention that, for far too long, they have needed and deserved.

Outside of the Ford Foundation, other beneficiaries of capitalism are also thinking about how we ought to improve our market system and address the root causes of inequality that are inherent within it. One inspiring example is Nick Hanauer, a successful entrepreneur and venture capitalist who has used his wealth and influence to reduce inequality by attacking it at its roots.

Nick made his fortune as a serial entrepreneur. His grandfather and great-uncle—fleeing from Nazi Germany—started a bedding business now known as the Pacific Coast Feather Company.[72] Nick grew up working in the family business, trying his hand at every odd job. Even though his family owned the business, he did physical labor and had to work his way up through the company ladder. Nick says this taught him the value of work. And though his career took off—as an early investor in Amazon, a starter and seller of multiple companies, and eventually the co-founder of venture capital firm Second Avenue Partners—he never forgot that lesson.

That's why Nick has been fighting to increase the minimum wage for years. In June 2014, in his hometown of Seattle, Nick was successful: He helped get an ordinance passed that put Seattle businesses on a timeline to incrementally raise their minimum wage to $15 an hour.[73] (Larger businesses had to move faster, while smaller businesses were given more time to adjust.) Perhaps most remarkable was that this minimum wage increase included tipped workers, for whom the federal government currently sets the minimum at $2.13.[74]

Years after this policy was enacted, Nick argues that it has been an unmitigated success. As he wrote in *POLITICO Magazine:*

> *When the ordinance passed in June of 2014, Seattle's unemployment rate already stood at a healthy 4.5 percent; in April 2017, it hit a record low of 2.6 percent (basically a labor shortage). Seattle is now the fastest growing big city in America. Our restaurant industry is booming, second only to San Francisco in the number of eateries per capita, with food service industry job growth far outpacing the nation. Restaurateurs who once warned against raising wages are now complaining about how hard it is to fill the positions they have.[75]*

The reason for all of this, Nick explains, is that raising the minimum wage gets at several root causes: systemic poverty, yes, but also a slowdown in our capitalist system. After all, if you pay people more, that means more people have money to spend in the marketplace. That means businesses get more customers—and, subsequently, need to hire more workers to meet that demand.

It's not a coincidence that this "virtuous cycle" produces a more just outcome.[76] As Nick put it: "The more fully we include people, the more just the market is, the more prosperity we get. Justice is the source of all prosperity."

Of course, much of the work Nick does on this front is not "charity" according to the US government, in that it's not tax-deductible the same way donating to, say, the American Red

Cross is. Philanthropists call this the difference between "c3" and "c4" donations. 501(c)3 organizations are tax-exempt charities, religious organizations, and educational organizations that do not have a partisan bent. 501(c)4 organizations are tax-exempt too, but they don't have to be nonpartisan. The catch: You can't get a tax deduction for donating to the latter.

But Nick argues that the wealthy shouldn't spend any time thinking about this distinction. In fact, it's a distraction from getting at root causes. As he told me, "I don't make a distinction between c3 and c4 dollars in my mental process. I don't count how much is deductible. All I think about is maximizing the amount of progress that I can make." Nick went on to explain: "I could donate a million dollars through my foundation in c3 to a homeless shelter, or I could use that same million dollars to run a campaign to raise a tax to generate $300 million a year to help with homelessness. For me, it's not even a close call."

There is, however, a downside to justice-oriented philanthropy: You may not win universal approval from your peers. "When you give $1 million to the homeless shelter, your wealthy peers congratulate you and the papers write a nice story about how generous you are," Nick pointed out. "When you use the same $1 million to run a political campaign to raise the taxes that it will take to actually address the problem of homelessness structurally, you get hate mail. You are shunned by your peers, and the newspapers call you a communist."

This can be a real challenge, especially for wealthy people. It creates conflict with their peers and requires some antagonizing. But we shouldn't be doing charitable works just to win approval, or to get along with everyone, or for the sake of a tax deduction. We should be deploying our resources to address the problems in whatever way is most powerful and efficient—regardless of how it may help us.

Obviously, addressing the root causes of injustice in this way does not mean we have to neglect the immediate needs created by those problems. In fact, we shouldn't neglect these symptoms; doing justice means addressing the underlying sources of injustice *and* their effects. The ways we can work along this continuum from the surface to the root causes—from generosity to justice— are exemplified in so many ways: from the work of the Equal Justice Initiative to the fight to raise the minimum wage to, on a more local level, the efforts of the innovative Brownsville Community Culinary Center.

Located in east Brooklyn, Brownsville is one of the borough's poorest and most dangerous neighborhoods. According to a 2017 report from the Citizens' Committee for Children of New York (CCC), it is the most hazardous area for children to grow up in in Brooklyn.[77] The neighborhood suffers from a scarcity of supermarkets, banks, businesses, restaurants, and public transportation. "What makes Brownsville unique is you have a scarcity of a whole slew of assets," Apurva Mehrotra, the CCC's former director of research and data analysis, told the *New York Daily News* in 2017. "It's not a mild scarcity."[78]

Determined to improve this fledgling community through food, Lucas Denton, a former ironworker and human rights activist, and Claus Meyer, a culinary entrepreneur, opened the Brownsville Community Culinary Center (BCCC) in June 2017.[79] This nonprofit organization offers a 40-week, paid culinary training program to local residents.[80] Program participants receive training in culinary arts, hospitality, financial literacy, personal budgeting, and time management, and many go on to work various jobs within the food industry.[81] Aside from being a much-needed job training facility for the community, the center is also a sit-down restaurant and café that offers healthy affordable food to local residents. When it opened in 2017, it was, according to residents, the first sit-down restaurant of any kind to open in Brownsville in 50 years.[82]

The BCCC serves many roles: culinary school, job training program, restaurant, community center. Its mission is to offer "healthy, accessible cuisine to neighborhood residents," to create a place that "educates and inspires participants to excel in the food-service industry," and to "serve as a forum through which the Brownsville neighborhood can address and organize around issues of food injustice."[83] Just as the Pathmark supermarket did after opening in Harlem two decades earlier, BCCC is increasing Brownsville residents' access to healthy food options; it is solving an immediate need. But it is also simultaneously tackling a root cause of the area's food scarcity: a lack of gainful employment opportunities.

As local residents graduate from the culinary program and secure lucrative food industry jobs, the buying power of the community will increase. As the community's buying power increases, not only will more businesses flock to the area, but local businesses already established there will be more successful. BCCC's intervention at the root of the problem will have a cascading effect that will foster both immediate and lasting change.

Ultimately, to solve the systemic causes of injustice, we must learn to both zoom out and zoom in. We have to remain aware of the larger issues at play as we craft on-the-ground solutions that address them. And we must understand that as we dig deeper and deeper to excavate these systemic causes, we may find that what was once a "root" solution isn't anymore. In 1999, addressing a root cause meant building a supermarket. Now, it's opening a community culinary center.

We constantly have to push ourselves to dig deeper, to excavate more. The root causes of injustice are often obscured—buried deep in our history, our institutions, and our cultural practices—and they are not singular. They are a tangled network of interrelated issues that feed and support the problems we see. Excavating them is an ongoing process that will require patience, commitment, and an understanding that the excavation process will not always look the same.

While one community may be struggling with a scarcity of business investments, another may be grappling with gentrification. Every community is different, and unique communities will require unique solutions. In order to craft programs and initiatives that effectively address systemic problems, we have to familiarize ourselves with those whom we are trying to help. If we don't take time to gain this knowledge, we risk crafting plans of action that don't truly meet the needs of the community. So, we must hear from those who have a keen understanding of the community's needs. To effectively formulate on-the-ground solutions that attack the root causes of injustice, we must first learn to listen to the people on the ground.

NURTURING
COMMUNITIES

A Conversation with Carly Hare

For years, Carly Hare has been working both on the ground, building and growing activist movements, and in philanthropic organizations, pushing them toward justice.

Throughout her career of public service, she has led organizations committed to improving the lives of underserved communities large and small. Today, she is the coalition director for CHANGE Philanthropy, a group that advocates for more equitable practices in the philanthropic sector.

As a woman and citizen of the Pawnee Nation, Carly has fought for the rights and well-being of Native peoples specifically, serving as executive director of Native Americans in Philanthropy and, prior to that, as director of development for the Native American Rights Fund.[84]

Carly has also volunteered her time to serve on a number of boards and advisory committees supporting various causes, including the Common Counsel Foundation (which supports groups that organize for environmental, racial, and economic justice)[85] and the D5 Coalition (which seeks to advance "diversity, equity, and inclusion in philanthropy").[86]

This unique vantage point allows Carly to both understand the world of philanthropy and see where charity isn't enough to help underserved communities. She has called for philanthropists "to move toward philanthropic equity" by making fundamental changes to the structure of charitable organizations. These changes include, but are not limited to, hiring "people from underinvested communities" at every level of an organization, and increasing investments in unrestricted resources within those communities so they can maintain decision-making power.[87]

In short, Carly is a philanthropist seeking justice, and a justice activist pushing for better philanthropy.

DARREN: Carly, could you describe yourself and the work you do?

CARLY: When I was 16, I received my Pawnee name in our traditional, communal, familial way. That name is <i kita u hoo <i]a hiks, which translates to "kind leader of men." So, in a way, I've always been called to have a space and play a role, even if that space and that role were not traditional. Because I come from a tribal community, the values of reciprocity, community-centered care, leadership, and wisdom-sharing are all very important to me. And those values are deeply embedded in the work that we do organizationally, and also in how I navigate the work personally.

I've been in philanthropy for such a long time now that I often find myself in a meeting thinking, *How am I the elder at this table?*

DARREN: Don't worry, you're not the elder here.

CARLY: But in some rooms, in certain crowds, I am! I've been doing this work for 15 years now. When I first entered the field, I felt a bit like an interloper. I spent a lot of time trying to demystify this field. But then, like most people, I went from feeling like an interloper, to feeling like an infiltrator, to feeling like an interrupter.

Today, I'm excited about the work we're doing at CHANGE Philanthropy. Our coalition has evolved over the years. There have been some big changes, and we've begun not only challenging and questioning philanthropy but making a statement and putting out a call to action. It's even in our name.

The shift in philanthropy that we want to see is about influence, about magnifying impact, and about changing traditional dialogues and practices—which is why this frame of approaching philanthropy through justice is so exciting to me.

Most people in philanthropy today are getting more comfortable with exploring these changes, and they're beginning to implement and practice some of them, so it's an exciting time to be in the field. We've been able to bring forward some of that wisdom that has always been present, in a more coordinated, strategic, and intersectional way. The deeper work we're focused on is about justice and liberation, and I'm interested in the role that philanthropy can play in that work.

DARREN: You've been at this for quite a while, and all your work has culminated in CHANGE Philanthropy. So why did you get involved? What was it about philanthropy that drew you to this work?

CARLY: I feel very fortunate to have had the entry point into this work that I did. I started working in philanthropy as a program officer at The Community Foundation Serving Boulder County. I was about 25 years old, and I was the only person of color on its staff at the time.

It was a wonderful challenge and a great experience. The president of that foundation hired staff based on our potential rather than strictly looking at our résumé and background. And I think that experience changed how I look at the world and the work of philanthropy. Back then, it took me three weeks of practice before I was even able to pronounce the words "philanthropy" and "philanthropist" without tripping over them. It was definitely a challenge. But some of the best advice I got was from my previous employer, who ran a Native-led organization. I sat down with him and told him about my new position. Without a pause he told me, "We need more people to learn about this work and share it with our community. Because we don't know that world, and we need to know more about it."

Not everyone has the kind of opportunity I did. These systems often don't have entry points designed for people like me. That was a big challenge.

So, the work that I'm involved in is the work that I'm personally connected to. The evolution of change is about shifting these access points. It's about broadening the pipeline, rethinking the structures, and understanding how different individuals and institutions are navigating this space. Our communities need us to go in, learn, figure out how to thrive, and then change the work and the institution itself. That's a powerful motivator for a lot of people who are called or invited or pushed into doing this work. And the most important thing is the ability to assess your surroundings, adapt to this environment, and then use the systems of power to your own advantage to shift the entire industry's practice.

DARREN: Can you talk about what you think the difference between charity and justice is, and how you practice the two in your own work?

CARLY: The way we think about it at CHANGE—and the way I think about it personally, when I'm working with colleagues or field partners—is that there's a broad spectrum from charity to justice, and different individuals and institutions occupy different bandwidths on that spectrum. We often forget about the edges of that spectrum. On one hand, we have charity-focused frames for grant-making. For many people who subscribe to that view, your investments and your engagement strategies often perpetuate the status quo.

There is a wide swath of foundations today that continue to support and engage with white supremacists and patriarchal systems. People like that, who are closer to the status quo, often aren't ready to have conversations with us. Their mode of thinking is very much rooted in that traditional charitable grant-making model for institutions and organizations. We're fully aware that it's going to take a lot of work—on both the individual and the institutional levels—to shift these people from a charity-focused model to a justice- and liberation-focused model.

But then, on the other end of the spectrum, there are the people who are focused on liberation—who want to move toward liberation-focused frames of funding, where foundations step away from the power dynamics of the past and pursue a more democratized approach that's centered on community. These individuals and organizations aren't focusing just on rectifying inequality, but on promoting a different vision for the field itself. And that's radical. They're interested in shifting our frames for understanding this work and this world, and in thinking about how we can modify our existing approaches.

I want to share one more thought on this point. There's a quotation that has guided a lot of my thinking on this subject. I can't remember who originally said it, but it's something like: "The American policies of termination and extermination weren't as detrimental to American Indians as the goodwill of white women."

I first encountered that idea when I was involved in tribal work—right before I made the shift into philanthropy. Aside from the sheer shock of the statement, what I take away from it is the fact that we can't find other people's solutions. It's something I think about every once in a while, especially when I'm in groups of mostly white women.

When we try to find other people's solutions, we inevitably cause new problems. Our intent and our impact are simply misaligned. That's why we have to be mindful to engage with the community. That's the difference between approaching philanthropy from a charity mindset and approaching it with a justice mindset.

It's easy to solve the problems that someone faces today with a quick Band-Aid solution, but you might create long-term consequences without realizing it. Caring about justice means being intentional about putting the voices of individuals and communities at the center of these conversations. It means making sure that these individuals have access to the conversations we're having about progress. It takes intentionality.

DARREN: A lot of what you're talking about gets at this question of root causes. As you say, none of these root causes will get addressed unless we speak to, engage with, and listen to the communities who are closest to the challenge and best positioned to know the solutions. So, when thinking about these root causes, what core underlying issues do you think we should be focusing on?

CARLY: The key, I think, is to address the core pieces of policy, or practice, that have created the disparities in our society.

When I was at Native Americans in Philanthropy, people would come up to me and ask, "How can we help address alcoholism in Indian communities?" They would tell me they didn't understand why American Indian communities had such low high school graduation rates, or why people in these communities were at such high risk for so many other dangers. And often my answer would be, "Well, have you ever heard of the Dawes Act of 1887[88]?" Because this single policy resulted in the disenfranchisement of American Indians across the country. It destroyed communities and leadership structures and shattered the foundation of so many communities.

Whether you're looking at education, community leadership, or other issues, we can name a number of individual pieces of legislation or policy that created the problems that so many communities of color face today.

Often, the issues we focus on in philanthropy don't address those root causes of isolation, whether it's the policing of our communities and our bodies, or the geographic or educational control mechanisms that have trapped so many communities. A charity-focused approach will never address those problems. People who are concerned with charity focus on whether kids will have food on the table tomorrow. It will focus on hiring truancy officers to track down students who don't show up to school. But it won't look at reforming the education system as a whole. It won't question what systematic disadvantages, say, a Latina woman might face on a daily basis.

So yes, a justice-centered approach means looking at those root causes. It means stepping back and owning our history—even the parts of it we're uncomfortable with. It means exploring how that history impacts us here and now, and identifying the pieces of policy or practice that created these systemic inequalities in the first place. It means reframing, refocusing, and realigning the work we want to see done. Sometimes it might mean making large-scale system modifications or taking approaches completely opposite to the ones we took before.

The people in our communities have those solutions. They have those ideas. They often don't have the luxury of the time, resources, or talent that we have in the philanthropy sector. To me, that's why we need to shift from charity to justice. But making that shift requires us to open our doors and think about the world differently.

If you're doing this work the right way, you shouldn't be thinking about what's a win for your institution; you should be trying to identify what role you can play in supporting solutions. It shouldn't be about the shiniest projects, or getting your name on things, or how this work will impact you. As individuals and institutions in this sector, we should be thinking about how we align ourselves with this work and the power that we hold.

DARREN: We all face obstacles as we attempt to take on this idea of a justice mindset in philanthropy. From your perspective, what do you think are the biggest challenges that you face when it comes to moving this justice mindset forward? What roadblocks have you encountered? How did you overcome them?

CARLY: One of the biggest challenges we face lies in the lexicon that we use. We share vague understandings of the concepts we care about, but we don't have shared core definitions of some fundamental terms.

What is equality? What is equity? What is justice? What is liberation? I hear people confuse equity and equality all the time, for instance.

Another challenge centers around the difficulties faced by people working within institutions. Last year, at our fall summit, we sort of coined a new term: "philanthrofolk." Essentially, it refers to the activists who are trying to shift the culture within their own institutions and move their organizations to a more equity-based mindset, as well as allies who are trying to support this work.

We realized that philanthrofolk aren't just fighting for access and opportunities to engage communities; they're also navigating the internal difficulties of the systems and institutions they operate within. For many of them, they might be the only voice within their organization that's pushing this conversation forward. That power dynamic presents daily challenges for them, and navigating it requires nimbleness.

We have to create and nurture dynamic communities. I'm so blessed that my work allows me to spend so much time with the communities that I love. I'm able to work in spaces where I'm supported personally, professionally, institutionally, programmatically, and economically. That's rare for folks in this field.

When I first started out in philanthropy, there weren't many Native Americans in the field; I knew only one other Native person who worked in philanthropy back then. Later, I found Native Americans in Philanthropy to be an instructional home for navigating this sector. I only got to see that group of people once or twice every year, but it still helped me feel as if I was part of a community. It brought me so much energy.

It's all about finding allies in the work. When I was in Boulder, Colorado, there wasn't a lot of Native work that focused on community foundations. But I was able to find that community while working with LGBTQ folks and Latinx folks. Isolation can be incredibly challenging, and forging those alliances helped a lot with that. Everyone needs that sense of community, where you can restore your soul. That space—whether it's virtual or physical—where you can be with people who are closely aligned with you is so important.

As the culture of the field shifts, those spaces are going to become more and more important, because people are going to need those connections. I remember the 2017 Unity Summit, where 15 or 20 people told me that they had been planning on leaving the field within the year. But finding their community, being a part of the community, and forming relationships with other people who are dedicated to this work helped them rejuvenate their commitment to being activists and agitators and champions.

At the same time, we also need to bring in new people who will help expand our own thinking—people who can expand our understanding of the world and challenge what we think we already know. If I had continued working exclusively in Native communities for my entire career, I could have done some powerful work. But my perspective has been deepened and my work has been strengthened by having conversations with leaders from a wide variety of fields, from LGBTQ organizing to immigrant and refugee work. Building solidarity among different communities and causes is what allows us to deepen our perspectives and create the kind of long-term systemic change that can only be accomplished with a collective approach. That gives me a lot of hope.

DARREN: What do you think donors need to understand to be better social justice philanthropists, especially when it comes to advocating for the kinds of communities that you work with?

CARLY: Be more open to revising your understanding of what the challenges and solutions for these communities look like. That can be an uncomfortable journey, and it requires a willingness to learn about the historical events that impact how we live today. Particularly if you're someone who has benefited from the injustices of the past, this might be difficult, but it's important if you want to make real change in these communities. Go in with an open mind and a willingness to learn.

Be with these communities and celebrate successes together. That success might look like achieving a successful policy reform, but it also might look like losing a ballot initiative but rejoicing in the community that you've built and the organizing work that you've done. Find those successes and celebrate them.

To that end, use the resources that already exist in your field. As I said, I'm very fortunate that I get to be in a position where I interact with these communities I love on a daily basis. But there are plenty of organizations you can partner with that are advocating for our communities and building bridges between our communities and philanthropy.

The thing I would most like donors and foundation executives to know is that this work is dynamic. It's complex. It's evolving. And if you are too hesitant to be in it—to evolve with it—then progress might be a little slower. But we will still move forward.

6

THE POWER OF PROXIMITY

VALUING BOTH EXPERTISE AND EXPERIENCE

My motto,
As I live and learn,
is:
Dig And Be Dug
In Return.[89]

— *"Motto,"* Langston Hughes

On a snowy winter day in 2014, I visited the Eastern Correctional Facility, a prison in rural Ulster County, New York. There I experienced a most astonishing and inspiring phenomenon: incarcerated men studying Latin, debating Greek tragedies, and speaking advanced Mandarin.

They recited the poetry of Langston Hughes and the essays of James Baldwin, and they looked just like me—mostly black and brown, from underserved and disadvantaged backgrounds. But they had determination and hope in their faces—a look of authentic confidence that follows only from hard-earned achievement.

These men were participants in the Bard Prison Initiative, the brainchild of founder Max Kenner and Bard College's brilliant president, Leon Botstein.[90] This pioneering degree-granting program for incarcerated women and men has been the recipient of Ford Foundation support for many years. As I visited with them— as I spoke with them about their wrenching accounts of bad luck, bad choices, and a criminal justice system that seems designed to rob them of their humanity—I felt heartbroken but also inspired.

In their stories, I was reminded of why the support of Ford and many other philanthropies, institutions, and people working on the front lines of social change matters so profoundly: Yes, inequality and injustice persist. But they are no match for the human spirit.

And I was reminded of something else too: There's no substitute for meeting people where they are, in the conditions they live in.

I knew all the facts and figures about incarceration in America. I knew a bit about incarceration on a more personal level, too, because I have seven cousins who've spent time in prisons in Texas and Louisiana. And I knew that systemic racism is one of the root causes of our mass incarceration problem. But I had to look these prisoners in the eye to understand the importance of bringing dignity into their lives. I had to hear them talk about Aristotle to see why the material conditions of prison life don't always have to do with material things. Those lessons are why I later encouraged Agnes Gund to visit the San Quentin State Prison in California.

Listening to the people closest to the problems themselves— the people affected by the issues you're trying to address, the

Philanthropy has to include all the actors. It has to include the people you intend to serve, the beneficiaries, the government—everyone. We think that philanthropy has to be much more about community-led development and ownership of the solutions, and so we perhaps take a little bit of a different view about the role of philanthropy. We recognize we're not at the center of the system; we are just one of the actors within the system, and we've got to be able to use our expertise to help create or help be a part of that collaboration.

—JEFF RAIKES, CO-FOUNDER OF THE RAIKES FOUNDATION

helpers already there who are trying to improve the situation—might seem like an obvious action to take. And yet philanthropists and activists of all stripes skip this critical step all the time. Why? What prevents us from seeking out the advice of those people who are close to the problem we hope to solve?

We know some of the possible reasons. Our privilege, for example, insulates us from the experience of many disadvantaged communities, limiting our perspectives and understanding. And our biases can keep us from seeing the value of other perspectives; our prior understanding and view can limit us to looking for people and organizations that already confirm our own beliefs and desires.

And on top of it all, our ego can cloud our judgment. We may mistakenly believe—as Andrew Carnegie seemed to—that we know what's best for others. Or we may think that we are the best suited to solve every problem, or that we will do it better than those attempting now.

These ingrained personal and institutional circumstances create upsetting, unhelpful power dynamics—the kinds that can foster a condescending and unproductive relationship between philanthropist and grantee.

And beyond these factors, other blockades and traps prevent us from listening—really *listening*—to the people who are affected by the problems we hope to resolve. Too often, organizations will go into a community expecting the community members to speak their "language," instead of listening to what those community members have to say. This was certainly my experience working at a Harlem nonprofit in the 1990s.

In the bubbles of our boardrooms, we develop a whole language of missions and metrics. And that's good and important. Measuring outcomes has value, as does knowing what you want to solve and what direction you're headed in.

We also turn to experts, which is important too. But we can easily fall into what the economist William Easterly calls "the tyranny of experts," putting too much weight on the strategic advice of the credentialed technocrats who often steer well-intentioned policy.[91]

Instead, in developing that strategy and those metrics, it's critical to listen to the people who experience these issues, and to put the problems and solutions in terms that match their lived experience.

The Bill & Melinda Gates Foundation, for example, learned this lesson with a grantee in a rural part of Ethiopia.[92] The grantee noticed that its treadle pumps weren't selling in some areas—even though these pumps were important to helping farmers irrigate smaller land plots. The problem—as the grantee discovered after talking to the women who weren't buying it—was that in order to operate the pump, one would have to stand on it and pedal with a movement that involved swaying one's hips. That motion violated cultural norms for women in the community. It didn't matter that the pump was effective—women farmers weren't going to buy it as long it required that kind of hip-swaying.

When the grantee redesigned the pump to avoid that motion, the pump became far more popular. But the problem was solved only because the grantee and the foundation consulted the people close to it.

Similarly, new entrants into philanthropy are often tempted toward what Jeff Raikes calls "silver bullets" and "silver units." As Raikes explained, "[The] silver bullet is that brilliant intervention: If everybody would just adopt this intervention, it's going to solve the problem." Sometimes the silver bullet solution comes from what Raikes calls the "silver unit": the "individual philanthropist or the singular foundation that thinks they have *the* solution."

The problem with silver bullets and silver units is, they almost never work. More often than not, if a problem had a silver bullet solution, someone would have tried it already. And for whatever problem or area you want to work in, it's always better to collaborate.

That doesn't mean you should avoid tackling big new problems or coming up with big new ideas. But taking wisdom from those who have been there before and learning how to leverage the people already working in your field can only benefit your cause.

Given all these barriers—of privilege and bias, of ego and strategy and silver bullets—how can we ensure that we're doing our best to listen to people closest to the problems? What steps can we take to ensure that we reap all the benefits of collaboration and context?

There are two powerful ways we can increase the odds that we'll really listen to the lessons of the people most: by practicing proximity and by extending empathy.

You might think that when I say, "Listen to people close to the problems themselves," I mean it in a metaphorical sense—that you should read about and solicit perspectives outside of your own. And that's a great practice. But in fact, I mean the phrase quite literally: You should *actually go* to the people and places you want to help. Walk around. Talk to people. Do so formally and informally. Meet the people you want to help face-to-face. Meet the people already there doing the helping, face-to-face.

Of course, getting up close and personal with people can get awkward or feel uncomfortable. Often, it means going to places that scare you or meeting people who are very different from you. But as David Rockefeller Jr. told me, "Through proximity, you enable yourself to lose the discomfort that comes from erroneous

> I feel a responsibility to use the wealth that I've inherited to empower people to have their own voice—to bring them to the table to participate, self-identify on their own terms, and be celebrated for who they are.
>
> —JON STRYKER, FOUNDER AND PRESIDENT OF THE ARCUS FOUNDATION

judgment." He's right. However uncomfortable you feel talking to someone of a different race, class, ability, or background, you'll feel even more uncomfortable if you get it wrong from the safety of an office.

When I spoke with Tricia Raikes, the co-founder of the Raikes Foundation, she also addressed the power of proximity:

> One of the antidotes to privilege is the notion of proximity. We probably can't punctuate that enough. I think to really deeply understand the issues and the problems that need to be addressed, philanthropists need to get as close to the issues as possible to address them authentically. That can mean personally getting into the field—ensuring your staff really make that a priority—and bringing in the voices of those who will bring wisdom to the table. Proximity or situatedness is such a central point to the work and to doing it well.

Tricia's point about personally getting into the field hits home for me. In fact, at the Ford Foundation, whenever we're unsure of how to solve a problem or why something isn't working, my first response is: Have we tried talking to the people close to the problem?

Being proximate also helps with the second strategy, extending empathy. Laura Arrillaga-Andreessen put it well:

> I would argue that equally important to proximity, and fully integrated into it, is having empathy for those we aspire to serve and to empower and to uplift. Empathy is the crux of design thinking, which is the framework I use for all the organizations that I've built and the resources that I've created. And it's essential not only

*for the functioning of philanthropy but also, I would argue, for
the functioning of our democracy and the evolution of our souls.*

Empathy is powerful because it's a step beyond sympathy. It's
not merely agreeing that the situation is challenging or needs fixing—it's seeing the problem from the perspective of the person
who experiences that situation. In fact, I'd take it one step further:
Real empathy is not just seeing. It's engaging all the five senses. It's
taking in the sounds and smells of a person living on the street in
poverty. It's feeling the pangs of an empty stomach or touching
the cold steel of a prison bar.

> Those of us who are willing to position ourselves in prox-
> imity to the poor, who understand how we're creating new
> narratives, who are willing to do uncomfortable things,
> who will endure some challenges and hardships—these
> are the ones, you are the ones, who will honor what it
> means to create a truly just community.
>
> —BRYAN STEVENSON, FOUNDER AND EXECUTIVE DIRECTOR
>   OF THE EQUAL JUSTICE INITIATIVE

Being proximate will help you engage your senses. And
extending empathy will help you turn those senses into insights.

When Ballmer Group decided to begin working in Detroit,
Steve and Connie Ballmer knew plenty of other donors and philanthropic interests were at play. So instead of just parachuting in,

they made a decision that was at once obvious and bold: They hired someone with strong roots in Detroit, who understood the city's communities and challenges, to help lead the program there.

That didn't mean they had to abandon their model. Ballmer Group cares a great deal about collecting data and using that data to generate ideas. So, it was a balancing act. As Connie said, "We would never come to a community and tell them what their outcome should be or what they should be working on. That's owned by the community. But we *can* have an opinion about how we have seen this work done most successfully and what elements of the work we would fund."

Hiring someone from the community you're working in—and putting that individual in a position of power—is a great first step. The next step is to move toward discomfort by putting yourself into the community itself.

Laurie Tisch—daughter of Preston Robert Tisch, the late part owner of the Loews Corporation—is the founder and president of the Laurie M. Tisch Illumination Fund, which offers grants for education, arts, service, and food access, among other causes.[93, 94] This point about the importance of discomfort and proximity is one Laurie makes often: It's hard to understand the human impact of a project when you're just reading about it on paper or talking about it in a meeting.

As Laurie said, "If we're doing more abstract things, it's hard for me to internalize it unless I really see it or somebody else [in the organization] has seen it. And that's reinforced every time I go—and not just go, but really talk to people."

Laurie offered a specific example from personal experience: the first time she visited an urban farm in New York City's public housing, built by Green City Force, an AmeriCorps program that gets young people who live in public housing to grow healthy food and to serve their country by being stewards of the environment.

> *I thought I was in Iowa. In these little patches of land, they're growing all these fruits and vegetables. I was at an opening at one uptown, and the corps members took me around. One asked, "Do you want to see where the stevia grows?" I said, "Oh, my God, I didn't know stevia grew. I thought it just came in little green packets." But these kids—they were probably 18 or 19 years old—not only were they just so proud about what they were doing, but they also really understood it.*

It was clear the visit had an impact on her view of the program. "I couldn't have read that," Laurie told me. "I had to see it."

Ultimately, listening actively to the people closest to the problems is about one thing: respect. By getting up close and personal, you will gain respect for the people you're working for and working with—like Laurie did.

What's more, by being involved and extending that respect, you'll get some back too. If you treat people like peers and partners in your process, the reward is a warmer welcome into the community—along with far deeper knowledge of the problems you're trying to address and what solutions are worth trying. And those advantages are critical if your ultimate goal is real lasting justice.

In short, respect spreads respect. As Langston Hughes might put it: If you dig, you'll get dug in return.

BRINGING HIDDEN LABOR TO LIGHT

A Conversation with Ai-jen Poo

For me, Ai-jen Poo's advocacy has always felt not only necessary, but personal. My grandmother was a domestic worker in Houston, Texas, and my mother was a nurse's aide while taking care of four children of her own at home. I know the labor of both women who raised me was too often undervalued—and sometimes even unseen. Ai-jen Poo has dedicated her life to illuminating the needs of such "invisible people." She partners with housekeepers, caregivers, and nannies—those who do, in her words, "the work that makes all other work possible."

Ai-jen co-founded Domestic Workers United (DWU) after listening to Filipina domestic workers speak about abuse they experienced at the hands of their employers. Initially, DWU developed industry standards and connected people to channels for legal recourse. But the organization eventually took its advocacy to the state legislature, where it successfully lobbied for New

York to adopt a Domestic Workers Bill of Rights that quickly became a national standard.[95] Ai-jen also co-founded, in 2007, the National Domestic Workers Alliance, an organization that has partnered with more than 60 affiliates to advocate for domestic workers.[96]

Ai-jen's brand of organizing has always been imaginative. She has fearlessly challenged fundamental assumptions in our society, in particular encouraging us to undo the patriarchal understanding of labor that often excludes those working in what she calls "the care economy."

DARREN: Can you talk about the work you've done on behalf of domestic workers, and explain your concept of the care economy?

AI-JEN: My work is about giving voice to, and bringing dignity to, the work that allows working families to go out and participate in the economy. We call it "the work that makes all other work possible." It's the nannies who care for our children, the housecleaners who maintain our homes, the elder care providers and the home care workers who take care of our parents and our grandparents, and who support our loved ones with disabilities. That work inside the home makes it possible for all of us to go out into the world and do what we do. And yet it is some of the most undervalued work in our economy, and historically it has been done by women of color and immigrant women.

In addition, the conditions of the work—long or unpredictable hours, lack of access to a safety net or benefits, lack of career ladders and pathways to career advancement—are increasingly the norm for too many American workers. It used to be seen as really conditioned at the margins of the economy. And now, more and more American jobs are becoming as vulnerable and as insecure as domestic work has always been. Just about everybody can relate to the need for care—whether it's child care or elder care or something else—and we deal with those pressures on top of the pressures of participating in the workforce without much support.

We're all caregivers, but we're doing it in isolation.

So, our organization tries to bring respect and security to this work, and point toward solutions that make the entire workforce more secure, more dignified, and more sustainable for families.

DARREN: Is that what justice looks like to you?

AI-JEN: Yes. Justice, to me, is an equal starting point for all of us in the economy. It looks like people being recognized and valued for their work and their contributions in the economy, and being able to earn a living and take pride in the work they do to support their families.

DARREN: How do you define your relationship to philanthropy? What does good philanthropy look like?

AI-JEN: I see my relationship to philanthropy as one of partnership, strategic coordination, and collaboration.

I believe leaders in philanthropy are going to play a huge role designing solutions that address some of the biggest challenges of our time. Philanthropic leaders—together with leaders in social change movements, in the field, and in the private sector and in government—are going to need to work together to effectively address the challenges that face us. No one sector can do it alone.

As much as I believe in the work that's happening on the ground in the field, we can't do it without our partners and our co-conspirators in philanthropy and in other sectors, because of what we're up against. The challenges and opportunities of the day are just too great.

DARREN: To you, what's the difference between charity and justice?

AI-JEN: One piece is that charity assumes a relation of power that doesn't shift. Charity is like a Band-Aid. It's getting you the resources and services and support to address an injury, but not actually getting at the reason for the injuries to begin with. How did you end up in the hospital? And what can we do about that? What can we do to shift power so that there's more equity and balance and humanity in the way the world works?

Agency is another way of talking about it: Justice is giving more people the agency to define and to make choices in their lives and our democracy.

DARREN: Of course, what a root cause looks like has changed over time too—from the more scientific ideas of Andrew Carnegie and John D. Rockefeller to our notions today of racism and sexism. In your work, what are some examples of root causes you are tackling?

AI-JEN: One root issue is the devaluing of care work, or certain forms of work that have been associated with women. That's a reflection of the patriarchy—the fact that we're still living in an economy where women are paid less for the same work, and

women of color even less. And meanwhile, work that has historically and culturally been associated with women, like caregiving
work or work in the home, struggles to be recognized as real work.

We've created a hierarchy of value in our economy that
reflects the way we value people. That's the root cause I'm trying
to address.

DARREN: The impact that you want to have may be around
work in the economy, yet there's clearly something deeper that
you want too. There's a hunger that comes from your work, and
your voice, for justice.

AI-JEN: At its heart, it's about recognizing the human dignity
and potential of every person.

DARREN: Closely related to that dignity and potential is the
power of privilege: You and I have been privileged relative to a lot
of the people we are seeking to work with. How do you see your
own privilege, and how do we extend the kinds of privileges that
you and I have to others?

AI-JEN: With privilege comes responsibility. We need to do a
lot of listening and learning to understand what to do with that
privilege.

I've heard you talk about proximity, and I think you're right
that it's important to remember our field of vision is defined
by our narrow set of experiences. So, the more proximate we
become to different kinds of people and experiences, the more
our field of vision expands to see the world in as many dimen-
sions as possible.

If our privilege can put us in proximity with enough people to have a fuller picture of the world, we can help people in privileged rooms see the world through the eyes of the people who are less seen.

DARREN: While you are this iconic person in our field, and in spite of what I just said about privilege, it hasn't been easy. From your standpoint, what are the biggest challenges you've faced, advancing this mission of human dignity and justice?

AI-JEN: One of the things I've just come to realize is that change is really hard for people. As human beings, we develop habits and patterns because they help us make meaning and secure ourselves in an uncertain world. Something that has surprised me over the years, even in the social change sector, is how reluctant we are to change and how fearful we can be of it.

But without a significant amount of disruption, there is no way that the people I represent are ever going to get justice. There is a profound amount of change that we're going to have to make, and it feels like a slow and uphill battle. Even though we have made historic progress, it feels like it never quite meets the moment.

DARREN: At the same time, there's something in your work that is very optimistic. How do you see optimism as an activist, especially considering the long slog and the series of successes and setbacks?

AI-JEN: Optimism is key. I find it impossible to be creative when I'm in a cynical mood. The times we are at our very best in terms of being generative and productive is when we're in a space of optimism and possibility. Optimism has to become a practice for us in order for other possibilities to emerge or reveal themselves, especially in dark times.

DARREN: Over the past ten years, what have you learned that has most profoundly impacted you, that you didn't know when you started this work? And how can other people apply what you've learned to their work?

AI-JEN: There is something important to be learned in every single room. And one of the great gifts of privilege has been the ability to be in meetings with all kinds of people: advertisers, creatives, entertainers, people in business and tech and the world of investment capital. In every single room that I'm in, I learn something profound that is related or relatable to what we're doing. And at the level of trying to retool and redesign society for equity, each of those fields of vision offers a vital perspective, even if you'll never fully understand that perspective just by going to a few meetings. Ultimately, the more you know about what you don't know, the better chance you have of designing an effective strategy.

And in every single one of those rooms, there are people who share our vision of equity and opportunity. I've been surprised and encouraged by how many bridges we've been able to build and how many people actually do care about what happens to domestic workers and what happens to the future of the care workforce. It's our shared humanity. That's a common starting point for how we collaborate and work together.

Finally, I've learned to center people who have the most at stake in some of the policies and systems and structures that we're trying to shape—people like the members we represent, the women who do this work every day—and to bring their experiences, their perspectives, their hopes, and their dreams into as many spaces as possible. It's beneficial for everyone. It's not just about it being the right thing to do, but actually the strategies get better. The conversation gets grounded in reality. And the solutions are much more impactful.

We call that "building power from the margins until the margins disappear." Not because we want to reinforce this margin-centered dynamic—which I often fear we sometimes do in our discourse when we talk so much about the marginalized. But we're bringing in the voices of the marginalized in such a way that it totally changes the dynamics until the margins no longer exist—until we're all at the same table, actually working on the same solutions.

DARREN: Sometimes donors don't really get why it's important to fund organizations like yours. Sometimes they might say, "Oh, well, they're not directly serving the poor. I want a direct service organization in my grant-making." What do you say to philanthropists who haven't come to understand or embrace why justice-seeking organizations, organizations like yours that talk about justice, ought to be a part of their portfolio of giving?

AI-JEN: My type of organization is trying to change the power dynamic on the issues. We're harnessing the creative potential and leadership of the people who have the most at stake in whatever programs philanthropy is investing in. And at the end of the day, it increases the impact of all of these strategic solutions and services. Absent an organization like mine, all of that human potential and perspective gets left on the table.

Justice organizations try to harness the energy where there are gaps—where the most disenfranchised or the least visible have the most at stake. Harnessing that creativity, that leadership, that energy improves the impact and design of our solutions.

DARREN: A lot of donors want to help vulnerable children—but many of those children are in families headed by the very women you are representing. Part of the reason those children are vulnerable is because their mothers are working in low-wage jobs. Donors need to understand that when they want to help vulnerable children, they have to help the parents of those children provide a standard of living through their income.

And we know from the research that people who are more economically secure are able to provide better parenting. And the reverse is true too.[97]

AI-JEN: That's right. The level of stress and disease and unhealthiness in a family is directly tied to economic security.

DARREN: So, while some may say, "Let's look for a direct service organization," if we actually paid these women a decent wage and they had fair working conditions, they could provide more stability for their children and families. It's an economic justice issue, but it's also a family security issue.

AI-JEN: And in the family economic security conversation, the question of wages and jobs and dignity and economic security for the adult-aged parents is never a part of the conversation, and it should be. It's fundamental to it.

DARREN: Yes, you're right to draw the full circle of justice and center it on the family and the essential need to have a decent wage for work. We have a problem that certain categories of work are devalued and underpaid, and that has implications for family security, community, efficacy, and social capital. So, somebody wanting to work on all these other issues needs to see your work as essential.

AI-JEN: Since reading your blog again, I've thought a lot about what a new approach to philanthropy for the twenty-first century looks like. The first "Gospel of Wealth" came about during another time of massive transformation in this country, in the middle of an industrial revolution. Inequality was severe, but change was happening on every single front. In those periods, which only come around once every few generations, it's almost as if history moves a little faster, and it requires also that we move a little faster. Unfortunately, philanthropy is kind of notorious for not moving very fast.

So, at this particular moment in history, as we look at philanthropy for the future, how do we rise to meet the kind of speed with which change is happening? How can we make sure we're at the table and being a positive force of catalytic change? We're in another one of those moments where history is moving so fast— which means we have a shot at making interventions in the name of justice that are much larger than average.

I've been doing this organizing for 25 years now. It's been an incremental slog for that whole time. And yet right now, it feels like we can actually do some really big things. But we need philanthropic leadership and partners to help us keep up and move faster.

7

THE COURAGE OF CONVICTION

STANDING UP AND SPEAKING OUT

The opposite of love is not hate, it's indifference.[98]

—*Elie Wiesel*

In 1970, Aretha Franklin was at the height of her fame. At just 28 years old, she had already been crowned the "Queen of Soul" for her string of soul hits, including "Respect," which had become both a crossover hit and an anthem for the civil rights movement. Despite living in a time rife with discrimination against black Americans, Franklin enjoyed mainstream success for her music, both at home and abroad. This widespread acclaim, however, did not prevent her from taking a public stand against injustice, even when doing so threatened her career.

On October 13, 1970, Angela Davis, a vocal social justice activist, was arrested in connection with a deadly escape attempt from a courthouse in Marin County, California.[99] Although Davis did not participate in the failed attempt to free three prison inmates thought to be wrongfully accused of murder, the guns used in the process were registered under her name. She was indicted on a string of serious charges, including murder. And when news of Davis's arrest made headlines, Franklin voiced her support. In a December 1970 statement to *Jet* magazine, Franklin said she was willing and ready to post Davis's bond "whether [it was] $100,000 or $250,000."[100]

This kind of public stance was extraordinary. Although Davis is celebrated today in some circles for her civil rights activism and her pursuit of social justice for the world's most marginalized communities, she was (and remains) a highly polarizing figure.[101] After her indictment, Davis went into hiding. She became the third woman in US history to join the FBI's 10 Most Wanted list. Shortly after her arrest, then president Richard Nixon praised the FBI for capturing "the dangerous terrorist, Angela Davis."[102] And it wasn't just a political issue; it was personal. Even Franklin's father didn't approve of her stance. Franklin said, "My daddy [Detroit's Rev. C. L. Franklin] says I don't know what I'm doing. Well, I respect him, of course, but I'm going to stick by my beliefs. Angela Davis must go free."

For Franklin to voice such outspoken support for Davis at this moment in America's history was beyond kind; it was courageous.

Offering to post Davis's bond could have greatly harmed Franklin's career, but she did not care. "I'm going to see her free if there is any justice in our courts . . . because she's a Black woman and she wants freedom for Black people," Franklin proclaimed.[103] "I have the money; I got it from Black people—they've made me financially able to have it—and I want to use it in ways that will help [Black] people."[104] Franklin will long be remembered as the First Lady of Soul, but even this well-deserved, accurate memorialization will not capture the full breadth of her legacy. She was far more than the Queen of Soul. She was a lover of justice who spoke out against what she saw as injustice, even when it wasn't safe to do so.

When we read and listen to the news today, it is hard to believe almost 50 years have passed since this incident. We are living in an eerily similar time. Hate and bigotry have made a dark and dangerous return to center stage in American culture. This troubling resurgence was most palpable in the days following the white supremacist march in Charlottesville, Virginia, in August 2017. The most insidious elements of American history—as much a part of our national character as the Constitution itself—announced themselves anew, and in the most disgusting and frightening ways.

Racist, anti-Semitic white nationalists marched without hoods, shame, or stigma. And as I watched the images emerging from Charlottesville, aghast, I worried that hate was being normalized in America once again.

In the weeks following, the American people affirmed, as they have so often, that from darkness comes light. By the thousands, and in cities across the country, they expressed that—in the activist Fannie Lou Hamer's perfect phrasing of the biblical verse—"righteousness exalts a nation, but sin is a reproach to any people."[105]

To me, it seems clear, not just in this alarming episode, but in the deeper history it has laid bare: America has reached another defining moment. We face a crisis—the next battle for the soul of this country, one that will play out on the battlefield of our collective consciousness.

What happened in Charlottesville was merely the latest tremor along fault lines that have been present in the American story since its founding—a reopening of wounds that have barely been treated and that never healed. Those wounds have remained unhealed, in part, because many of our leaders have failed to acknowledge and address this country's deep-seated struggles with racism, discrimination, and injustice. Whether it is rooted in a fear of alienating constituents and stakeholders, or in an unwillingness to deride systems and hierarchies of power that they themselves benefit from, their silence has been stark and deafening.

In the not-too-distant past, the American people would turn to their elected leaders—especially the president—for guidance and moral clarity. Today, in a vacuum of such moral leadership, fear tempts many Americans to hunker down, protect themselves and their interests, and withdraw for the purposes of safety and self-preservation.

To make matters worse, even our most honorable leaders are neither incentivized nor encouraged to make decisions based on what they know is right. Rather, they operate in—and are constrained by—systems and narratives that reinforce historical inequalities and perpetuate the status quo. Our entrenched structures push leaders to be averse to precisely the moral leadership they should embrace.

The most obvious example is in government.

It's not controversial to say that our elected officials often are discouraged from putting nation ahead of party. In gerrymandered districts, they face retribution and primary challenges as retaliation for bipartisanship. With post-Watergate campaign finance regulations obliterated, they are forced to spend far too much time fundraising, fearful of money pouring in to oppose them. The result is a broken set of incentives—all of which discourage bipartisanship and deter our government representatives from tackling the real problems facing the people they represent.

In the private sector, meanwhile, corporate CEOs are mired in a system that often compels them to subordinate their personal values and beliefs. Yes, some have raised their voices—and this is progress—but too many feel pressured to focus on quarterly earnings and share prices at all costs, rather than enter moral debates or consider the human costs of their silence or support. Why risk offending consumers, analysts, or stockholders by taking a stand, especially when the stock market is riding high?

I think the idea that a company's only social responsibility is to increase profits for the stockholders is incorrect. I was recently interviewed by *Harvard Business Review*, where I tried to argue that businesses exist to serve society's needs, not simply shareholders; that society gives us a license to operate, and that we need to ensure that we are behaving and operating our businesses in a way that brings benefit back to society.

—KEN FRAZIER, CEO AND CHAIRMAN OF MERCK & CO.

The obsession with and the American addiction to short-term gain—at the expense of long-term good—is the most obvious example of a larger phenomenon: leaders who make the trivial into the important and the important into the trivial.

In philanthropy and civil society, we too have been slow to recognize the ways our systems discourage moral leadership. Foundations often hide behind the particulars of our mission, rather than stand up for the deeper values our mission embodies. We keep our heads down to avoid making our organization a target for criticism, especially in the era of social media warfare.

The Ford Foundation is not immune to these trends, nor am I—and I know we must do better. I often wonder whether the foundation uses its voice in the most effective way. I question whether I have inadvertently contributed to these problems or reinforced these entrenched systems.

I know many nonprofit leaders and university presidents face similar challenges. They worry about offending their wealthy donors. Some feel constrained in their ability to speak out. They have my empathy, because every day these leaders walk a tightrope to address the diverse and often conflicting perspectives of the constituencies they serve.

Even though these problems feel particularly acute in the United States, I see these trends on every continent where we work. From exclusionary populist movements to attacks on public institutions, the media, and the very idea of knowable facts, the challenges we face are global—and so is our crisis of leadership.

While systems conspire to constrain us, the only acceptable response is courage—the moral courage to reject and rewrite the old rules. It was from the steps of the United States Capitol, in the presence of presidents and with hope for the future, that Maya Angelou proclaimed,

> *History, despite its wrenching pain,*
> *Cannot be unlived, but if faced*
> *With courage, need not be lived again.*[106]

In the end, practicing a New Gospel of Wealth—unearthing the root causes of injustice—will require us to exhibit the same level of moral conviction Aretha Franklin showed us in 1970: We must be willing to champion the cause of justice, even when it is risky for us to do so.

Speaking truth to power will always involve risk, even for those in positions of power. As Laura Arrillaga-Andreessen told me, "Pursuing justice—pursuing any major social change—entails taking immense risk. It entails making yourself vulnerable to criticism, to potential failure, to positional forces." Fortunately, however, we are not alone in this fight, nor do we lack guiding lights. There are leaders, both past and present, who exemplify what it means to pursue justice in the face of risk.

In spite of the disincentives facing CEOs—the pressures from consumers, shareholders, and boards—we've seen many industry leaders stand up and use their power, like Ken Frazier of Merck and Tim Cook of Apple (who frames the obligations of corporations as a "moral responsibility").[107]

In spite of criticism from other public officials, many elected leaders and university presidents have acted swiftly and courageously to remove Confederate monuments and address the uncomfortable truths of our history. In 2015, when South Carolina's then governor Nikki Haley removed the Confederate flag from the statehouse grounds, she noted that "this is a moment in which we can say that that flag, while an integral part of our past, does not represent the future of our great state."[108] Mayor Mitch Landrieu of New Orleans reminded us, in his now-iconic 2017 address on the removal of similar monuments, that "now is the time to come together and heal and focus on our larger task."[109] Others, like Gregory L. Fenves, president of my alma mater, The University of Texas, have done away with their communities' own monuments to our country's racist past.[110, 111]

In spite of the risk-averse cultures of many foundations, leaders like Jim Canales of the Barr Foundation and Grant Oliphant of The Heinz Endowments, among others, have offered powerful words rebuking the hate we saw in Charlottesville. Their admirable responses inspire me, as important examples of how we can speak truthfully and forcefully.

And in spite of many personal risks, leaders around the nation and the world are organizing and advocating for human rights for those who have been rendered invisible, exploited, and silenced by history. I'm talking about the moral courage of people like Fatima Goss Graves, president and CEO of the National Women's Law Center, and Sherrilyn Ifill, president and director-counsel of the NAACP Legal Defense and Educational Fund. I'm talking about Farhana Khera, president and executive director of Muslim Advocates, and Reverend Dr. William J. Barber II, leader of a powerful moral movement for justice. I'm talking about the courageous young people known as the Dreamers, who contribute every day to the only country they have ever known.

These leaders are my reason for hope in this time of peril. They demonstrate how we might fill the moral void at the top of our government and dismantle the systems that stifle progress on the ground. They remind us of what is possible when our political leaders, corporations, nonprofit organizations, foundations, and neighbors take up the mantle and choose to lead.

We need more like them.

We need leaders who build bridges, not walls. We need leaders who work across party lines and bring us together, not politicians who degrade our discourse and drive us apart. We need leaders who transcend the politics of division—who reject the language of exclusion even though it has proved to be a powerful political tactic.

It is up to each and every one of us to stand up for what is right—stand up to our boards and shareholders and political parties, and to our friends and colleagues, if necessary—even when it is not in our immediate interest. And we cannot wait. We must be the leaders our countries need and the world deserves. After all, what is the point of leadership if not to lead in times like these? What could we possibly be holding on to, or out for, when everything—*everything*—is at stake?

I remain ever hopeful. I firmly believe that those who wish to build a fair, more just world far outweigh those who desire the contrary. Every day, I encounter individuals who are exhibiting moral courage in both word and deed. They assure me that we can do this righteous work, that we can push ourselves forward on this journey toward justice, regardless of the obstacles.

Now is the time for courage. This is our moment to show each other—and the world—that we can rise above the flaws and mistakes of our past, that we are better and stronger than hate, fear, and injustice. Many challenges lie ahead, but if we remain ready and eager to lead the way toward a righteous world defined by its commitment to justice and fairness, we can overcome them. We can, at last, constitute a world that is truly worthy of our promise, and the promise of generations yet to come.

A CEO SPEAKS FOR JUSTICE

A Conversation with Ken Frazier

In August 2017, when white nationalists marched in Charlottesville, Virginia, the display was shocking, the violence horrifying. For many, the administration's lack of clear condemnation was appalling. For Kenneth C. Frazier, the CEO and chairman of the board of the biopharmaceutical giant Merck & Co., Inc., it was a call to action.

Ken took a public stance against hatred: He was the first to resign from the president's American Manufacturing Council. It was a demonstration of remarkable moral courage.

But for Ken, justice is not just something to stand up for in times of crisis; it is something he has been working toward and lifting up his entire career.

Before entering the C-suite, Ken defended people wrongfully sentenced to death, teaching black law students in South Africa and coming face-to-face with inequality. Since rising to the top at

Merck in 2011, Ken has been adamant about carrying on the tradition of the company's founder, pointing out that "the concept of medicine is for people; it's not for profit." And his focus on the genuine awareness of the needs of others, of putting people first, has been a guiding principle for much of his decision-making.

Many of the people I interviewed for this book are primarily philanthropists; Ken stands out as a business leader. As one of only three African American CEOs in the Fortune 500,[112] Ken has a unique view on the responsibilities that come with wealth and power, and the obligation we all have to champion the cause of justice. At the same time, his family's journey—from his grandfather, who was born into slavery, to his working-class parents, to his business career—traces American history and the uneven march of progress and gives him a special understanding of inequality and injustice. He is an inspiration to many and an example for all.

DARREN: Could you describe yourself, the work you do, and what you think makes the world a more just place?

KEN: My business card says that I am the chairman and chief executive officer of Merck, which is a company that's existed for 127 years, providing health care to people around the world.[113] That's my current responsibility and what I do.

But as a lawyer, ingrained in me is the fight for justice.

From my perspective, justice is about working on eliminating the root causes of poverty and discrimination. That is different from charity, which is more about dealing with the symptoms of these issues. Merck is deeply focused on corporate responsibility—much of it tied to helping address social inequalities.

An issue that we're very engaged with was recently on the cover of *The New York Times Magazine:* maternal mortality in the United States. Across the country, black women are three to four times more likely to die during pregnancy and childbirth than white women.[114] They are three times more likely to suffer from life-threatening complications.

The question is: How do we at Merck use our scientific and medical skills to address some of the foundational issues that could help stop so many of our mothers from dying? Some of it has to do with improving the disparities in health care, as well as working to ensure that African American women are afforded the basic standard of care and respect due to any person. The gaping disparity these women face, as the article put it, "has everything to do with the lived experience of being a black woman in America."

DARREN: Ken, you operate at a very high level in this society, and often when people talk about root causes, they don't name, say, racism. Do you think a lot of people would be uncomfortable still with addressing the real root causes of injustice?

For example, the real root causes are often these legacies that remain with us. A lot of people, particularly wealthy people, will say, "America's the land of opportunity! What's the problem?"

KEN: There are a couple of issues you just touched on.

The main one is the narrative we tell ourselves to explain how society works. Many "successful" people are invested in the concept that society is uniformly fair and meritocratic. Therefore, they feel their achievement in life is simply the result of hard work and talent. They're much less willing to look at the structural systems in play that cause some people to have greater opportunity. So, for many, equality is about having the same finish line. It's not always about having the same starting line, if I could use that metaphor.

Take education. I will tell you, in my own life, I have had tremendous luck. When I was a kid in Philadelphia, there was an effort around school desegregation, and I was one of the few children from the inner city put on a bus and made to ride 90 minutes a day—over my strenuous objections! I received a much more rigorous education than my next older sibling. While the social engineers of the city likely achieved what they set out to do in terms of letting a few black kids into white schools, they didn't deal with the more systematic and broad problem of the lack of quality education in the inner-city schools. That's an example of the opportunity gap being closed in my own situation.

I think the other issue, for all of us, is awareness. We're often just not conscious of what's going on around us. If we were enlightened to these structural and institutional issues—these historical legacies—then we could better solve those problems. But it's easier to write a check. It's easier to address the immediate need than it is to try to deal with some of these other issues, which, frankly, we haven't talked about in our society.

I used to teach in South Africa. Nelson Mandela, of course, deserves a lot of credit for keeping that country together through his personal example. But equally important was Archbishop Desmond Tutu's Truth and Reconciliation Commission, which got the historical issues of race and justice on the table in ways that, in this country, we still haven't. We largely avoid them.

DARREN: That's right. It's interesting because one of the messages of the National Memorial for Peace and Justice is all about the South Africa model. But as Archbishop Tutu argues in *No Future Without Forgiveness*, you can't have reconciliation if you can't have truth first.[115]

KEN: We don't have it here. I remember a case involving desegregation in Seattle, which the chief justice of the United States voted to strike down, saying our history is one of not making racial distinctions—that the way to end racial discrimination is simply not to discriminate. He basically said you shouldn't be able to use race to integrate schools anymore, which is ridiculous when you think about it.

DARREN: So, in your work and in your own way, how do you address these problems? You have already, in a pretty bold way, shown some real moral courage. And when you have someone like you in the corporate world, I hope that makes it easier for other people to be morally courageous CEOs and philanthropists. Do you see that? Or do you see resistance to that?

KEN: I see a huge amount of hesitation, which is understandable to some degree. Most corporate leaders don't want to have to take a moral stand. They're much more interested in the pragmatic benefits associated with being uncontroversial.

There's an element that says that you, as a CEO, have no right to take a moral stand because it's not necessarily in the best interests of the institution you serve or the shareholders. Again, people may be looking solely at the short-term benefits associated with maintaining advantage in our society. They're not looking at the long-term detriment to society that comes from those structural disadvantages, and how those disadvantages can create all kinds of problems because of instability. So, I don't think most corporations are interested in taking a moral stand.

I feel very fortunate to work for a company that has, as part of its own value set, a belief based on the concept articulated by our modern-day founder George W. Merck: "Medicine is for the people—not for the profits."[116] We're not exempt from our responsibility to shareholders, but we've always had the point of view that one of the most important ideas is equity in health. We have to make sure that we're doing our part, as a company, to direct our efforts. So it's not only "Let's give this person medicine because they're sick today," but also "How do we address the root causes of sickness and the root causes of health injustice in our society?"

If you want to promote social change, you have to think about change at a fundamental level.

DARREN: You've provided legal representation to men who were incarcerated. In fact, there was one man who was wrongfully incarcerated and facing the death penalty, and your intervention changed the course of his life. Where did you learn this idea of looking for justice? How did you come upon that as a focus?

KEN: It was two things. First, I was raised in a household where there was a religious overlay to everything that was happening. My grandmother was teaching us Bible stories, scripture stories— like the story of Exodus, with the Egyptians enslaving the Jews, and analogizing that to the situation that exists in our country. Or teaching us, as in Matthew 25:40, that whatever we did for the "least of these brothers and sisters," we did unto Him.

Second, I came of age at a time when America was grappling with these issues, with heroes like [Supreme Court justice] Thurgood Marshall and Bill Coleman—a mentor of mine who recently passed away, who helped write the legal briefs Marshall used to build his argument in *Brown v. Board of Education*. We were seeing people like Martin Luther King Jr. and listening to Malcolm X. Those individuals were taking on issues and forming my attitudes, because the country was grappling with its inconsistencies—between all the soaring rhetoric of Thomas Jefferson and the founding fathers and the reality of what was really happening.

So, that's why I became a lawyer. When I entered law school, I didn't know anything about representing big companies. I thought lawyers were social activists like Marshall, who said, "None of us got where we are solely by pulling ourselves up by our bootstraps. We got here because somebody . . . bent down and helped us pick up our boots." It's that sense that all of us who have benefited have a responsibility to not just give temporary help to people, but actually help address the questions: Why are people poor? Why are people discriminated against? Why are people not given the right level of education? I was always taught that you have to ask the deeper questions.

DARREN: For you and your wife and your families, when you think about your own giving, what do you prioritize?

KEN: For us, there's one very strong area of priority, and that is education. My wife was raised in Harlem; I was raised in North Philly. We both have the same experience of being sent to the better schools. It's hard to reduce one's life to a single variable, but I know in my case, as I mentioned earlier, it was being bussed from the inner city to nearly all-white schools that made this possible. The ambient standard of education in those schools was so much higher than it was in my local schools.

Coming back to Merck, and sitting where I do in this company today, I am focused on our responsibility toward giving. I find myself asking: What kind of health care system globally allows it to be the case that poor children are more likely to die before they're five years old? And how can we work alongside others to create better approaches?

That last question is the right question, and it's the one that we are increasingly moving toward asking. Why is individual health so dependent on accident of birth? When I talk with my colleagues about these issues, I say, "We were really smart when we picked the right mothers to be born to."

DARREN: What is it going to take to have more businesses and more business leaders speak up? Is it moving away from this relentless paradigm of shareholder value? Is it the way you talk about things in more of a stakeholder paradigm? What is that going to take?

KEN: I think the idea that a company's only social responsibility is to increase profits for the stockholders is incorrect. I was recently interviewed by *Harvard Business Review*, where I tried to argue that businesses exist to serve society's needs, not simply those of shareholders; that society gives us a license to operate, and that we need to ensure that we are behaving and operating our businesses in a way that brings benefit back to society. That's my own personal view. Having listened to a lot of discussions in the business world, I worry people are not thinking about things that way.

I think corporations have the responsibility to try to address some of the world's greatest challenges. Ultimately, if you want to solve the big problems that the world has—I'll just stay with health care—only a company like Merck can address them in a sustainable way.

DARREN: So that really does mean that you've got to become better partners with government, with the private sector, with philanthropists and NGOs. Everyone has a role to play in solving that problem.

KEN: I agree. None of us should rest until we've found ways— and I'm just going to stick with my business—to get these life-saving vaccines and therapeutics to people. Take HIV/AIDS, for example: if you live in the Western world, and you have means, it's a chronic, manageable disease. If you live in sub-Saharan Africa, it can still be a death sentence. And that shouldn't be the case.

DARREN: What would you say to emerging CEOs, C-suite folks, and philanthropists? What kernel of wisdom would you give them on their journey, as you look back on your own journey as a philanthropist, as a CEO, as a leader who has clearly exerted moral leadership?

KEN: Those of us who are in these positions—who are privileged to have resources and have control of these institutions—need to think deeply, dig for root causes, and be willing to upset the status quo. I think you have to be bold. I think you have to be courageous.

There needs to be a constant willingness to question the narrative about, for example, this country, and it being a place where everyone has an equal opportunity—well, we know that's not true.

How do we tilt the scales toward justice? The challenge is, charity is admired. It is socially acceptable. Seeking justice is controversial. It is politically, socially, and economically a huge risk to push for justice.

That's what I learned by saying what I said after Charlottesville. Some people thought I had no right to say that because they thought I was going against the president or not supporting what the president was doing. They were ignoring the underlying content, and I was actually surprised at how few business leaders wanted to step into the breach until they all felt like it was safe to go into the water together.

DARREN: That's right. You created a safe space. But without your courage, they would not have taken a stand.

KEN: I think that's right, and I think that's why I said people are not admired for seeking justice. That includes the people who are on the streets for Black Lives Matter or the #MeToo movement or the kids at Parkland or Dr. King from a Birmingham jail.

Those people are considered troublemakers in the way that Jesus was considered a troublemaker in his day. He was going around throwing the moneychangers out of the temple, and as a result they would rather spare a murderer, Barabbas, than spare Jesus.

At the end of the day, it comes back to awareness. If you listen to what Jesus said when he was hanging on the cross—and

I don't mean to be too religious—he said, "Father, forgive them, for they know not what they do." He was saying they actually think they're enforcing your laws. They don't understand the fundamental injustice of the world.

There's a lot in the scriptures about how we should be spending our time working on behalf of the needs of the oppressed. There's a line in Isaiah that is like poetry to me: "If you spend yourselves in behalf of the hungry and satisfy the needs of the oppressed, then your light will rise in the darkness, and your night will become like the noonday."[117]

We must address the needs of those people, and those needs are not just temporary or short-term needs. The fight for justice is never easy, but as a society, this is the most important fight we have.

8

THE DEMOCRACY OF JUSTICE

OUR LIBERATION IS BOUND TOGETHER

We need a Movement not for the poor but with the poor.[118]

—*Reverend Dr. William J. Barber II*

In the winter of 2018, I met with someone whom politicians, talking heads, and members of the media had called an "idiot,"[119] "ungrateful,"[120] one of many "suckers,"[121] and "an un-American jackass."[122]

For my part, I found Colin Kaepernick, the NFL quarterback who took a knee to protest police brutality and racial injustice, to be full of grace and wisdom. And I would give him a different list of names: protester, philanthropist, and patriot. In fact, he is one of the most patriotic people I have ever had the privilege of coming to know.

Those who call activists un-American forget that America was born from protest. The Declaration of Independence was not just a defense of the right to dissent and demonstrate—an excuse to dump chests of tea into a harbor—it was an expression and exclamation of that right. After "a long train of abuses," it explains, our founders "let Facts be submitted to a candid world."

This started a long history of American protest, which followed the model set by our founding fathers, of pairing symbolic acts with righteous words to call attention to the injustice around us.

It started a long history of something else, too: pushback by those in power, and resentment toward those who would dare question the status quo.

The Sons of Liberty destroyed British property and cried, "No taxation without representation." They were condemned by many colonists at the time, including George Washington.[123] Alice Paul and the National Woman's Party picketed the White House, carrying signs recalling Jefferson's words: "Governments derive their just powers from the consent of the governed."[124] They were arrested. Rosa Parks, too, was arrested for refusing to give up her seat—as were the patrons at the Stonewall Inn, before the riots broke out that sparked our modern LGBTQ rights movement. Justin Dart Jr. and countless other disability activists worked for years to support the American Disabilities Act (ADA) and the Individuals with Disabilities Education Act.[125] But in 1995, a mere five years after the ADA was passed, Dart had to resign all of his leadership positions to serve as a "full-time citizen soldier" to fight back conservative calls to repeal both pieces of legislation.[126]

What all of these patriotic protests have in common is a desire to wrestle with the founding contradiction of our country. On one hand, we extoll the ideas and ideals that inform our grand experiment in self-government. On the other, Americans constantly have fallen short of these ideals. We have fallen short since the beginning, and we continue to do so today.

One sad fact of history is that while we must demand our right to peaceful protest, we cannot always expect it. From Seneca Falls to Selma to Stonewall, the expansion of human rights and dignity is most commonly met with derision—often paired with violence, state-sanctioned or otherwise.

As someone whose love for my country is unwavering, I consider it to be the height of bravery and the definition of patriotism to protest injustice. To protest in America is ultimately an act of love for your country. Some risk life and limb to point out how America can and must be better. And despite the danger and what some might see as disrespect, I take solace in the fact that over time, to paraphrase an aphorism that is attributed to Mahatma Gandhi, those who oppose justice always lose. Always.

And while Colin Kaepernick is a wonderful example of a patriot, the power of his protest is also useful for understanding something else: You don't need money to do justice.

Of course, Kaepernick—as a former star quarterback—is wealthy.[127] And following his potent protest, he has become a leading philanthropist. Starting in September 2016, Kaepernick pledged to donate "one million dollars plus all the proceeds of my jersey sales from the 2016 season to organizations working in oppressed communities."[128] And he did, donating to causes as diverse as Black Veterans for Social Justice, reproductive health, climate change, and the free Mni Wiconi Health Clinic being built on the Standing Rock Sioux Reservation in the Dakotas.

But Kaepernick's philanthropy, while extremely commendable, is not the biggest contribution he has made toward justice.

Instead, his biggest contribution is recognizing the power of his platform to ignite a national conversation. He's now the face of Nike, inspiring millions of young people around the world to stand up for what they believe in—"even if it means sacrificing everything."[129] And that's because he saw that the most formidable action he could take for the cause of justice would be to, at the right moment in time, get down on one knee.

A shortcoming of Andrew Carnegie's "Gospel of Wealth" is that it is directed primarily at those with surplus riches. The central question of the gospel is simple: "What is the proper mode of administering wealth after the laws upon which civilization is founded have thrown it into the hands of the few?"[130] It is, no doubt, a good question. And one might argue it's not a flaw that Carnegie ignores those without wealth; it simply wasn't his project.

But by asking this question about administering wealth, Carnegie implicitly acknowledges that there is a problem with accruing massive amounts of wealth. In fact, he acknowledges it explicitly too, saying it is "the most injudicious" for men to, for example, "leave great fortunes to their children."[131] But this objection

> One of the things that I began to realize over the past 15 years is that you have to make your life philanthropy, in the sense that the greatest philanthropy doesn't always involve money. In fact, when all you can use is money, you see its incredible limitations.
>
> —STRIVE MASIYIWA, FOUNDER AND CHAIRMAN OF ECONET WIRELESS GROUP

exposes a contradiction that Carnegie fails to address: If passing on wealth is so injudicious, then what makes accruing it okay? Why should we ignore the massive inequality generated by the status quo? And why are only those who can take advantage of the current system—using their power and privilege—entrusted with redistributing wealth?

This attitude—that economic value supersedes all other kinds of value—is one of the more insidious forms of inequality. And unfortunately, it infects much of our public discourse today.

For example, I'm often forced to defend the economic benefits of having a thriving public arts sector in our society—even though the truth is, the value of art far exceeds the contributions it makes to our economy. Yes, funding the arts creates jobs and markets— but I support the arts because of its power to inform and inspire.

When I was just a little boy, I remember flipping through the glossy art catalogues that my grandmother, a domestic worker for a wealthy family, brought home with her. I was transfixed by the magic I saw on those pages—by images of worlds to which I had no other exposure. Those pages unlocked my capacity to imagine a world beyond my own—and to imagine my place in it. At that moment, I didn't care about how many people the arts economy employed. The power of the arts went far beyond that.

So, when Carnegie conveniently ignores the systemic problems that cause this great inequality of wealth, he is not just being classist; he is overlooking the power people have beyond their economic means. This raises a larger, more important question: What can *everyone* do, regardless of wealth, to make our system more just?

This question is posed to me often, in various forms. Most commonly it goes something like this: "Darren, I'm not a wealthy person. I don't have piles of money lying around. All of this charity and justice stuff—how does it apply to me?"

The answer is simple: No matter your level of income, in some way in your life, you are privileged—and that is a wonderful thing.

That may mean that you are privileged to, for example, have a beautiful singing voice. Maybe it means you can cook a delicious meal. Perhaps you are lucky enough to have a close group of friends. These privileges may seem irrelevant to the project and cause of philanthropy, but they are all critical: We need singers to entertain us at rallies and keep our spirits high after a hard day of fighting for justice. We need cooks to prepare meals for volunteers who are putting their bodies on the line for justice. And we need people with networks of close friends to activate them and ensure that as many people as possible are engaged in our projects.

Believe it or not, you don't have to donate a cent to be a philanthropist. As Elizabeth Alexander reminded me, the word "philanthropist" comes from the Greek for "loving mankind." And to be a lover of humanity, all you need to do is donate whatever privilege you have to the cause. As Laura Arrillaga-Andreessen puts it at the beginning of her book, *Giving 2.0*, "A philanthropist is anyone who gives anything—time, money, experience, skills, and networks—in any amount to create a better world."[132]

At the same time, it's not enough to just want to help. It's also important to see the bigger movement—and to find your place in it. A group of Australian Aboriginal activists in the 1970s, including the well-known artist and activist Lilla Watson, put it best: "If you have come to help me, I don't need your help. But if you have come because your liberation is tied to mine, come let us work together."[133, 134]

So, what does that look like in practice? Well, I think we might take inspiration from two people leading a movement that is explicitly *by* and *for* people without economic wealth: Reverend Dr. William J. Barber II and Reverend Dr. Liz Theoharis.

In April 2013, Reverend Barber, then the head of the North Carolina NAACP, walked into the North Carolina legislature with a plan: to peacefully pray and subsequently get arrested. He, along with 16 others, was charged with "trespassing" and "failure to disperse."[135] This particular protest—part of a movement that had grown since 2007—kicked off a nationwide series Barber called "Moral Mondays."[136] Every Monday, more and more protesters would show up and disrupt what they believed was an unjust political process that targeted the poor. More arrests were made. And more attention was drawn to their cause.

The movement soon spread, first to neighboring states Georgia and South Carolina. Then Moral Mondays protests popped up in Alabama and Arkansas, New York and Florida, Wisconsin and Indiana, Pennsylvania and Tennessee, Illinois and New Mexico.[137]

After several years of protests and pray-ins, marches and statements, Moral Mondays evolved into what is now called the Poor People's Campaign: A National Call for Moral Revival. The movement—named after a campaign led by another famous reverend who peacefully protested for civil rights—is now "uniting tens of thousands of people across the country to challenge the evils of systemic racism, poverty, the war economy, ecological devastation, and the nation's distorted morality."[138]

The first Poor People's Campaign famously set up a camp on the National Mall for six weeks in 1968 to protest racial and economic injustice. So in 2018, the new campaign spent six weeks leading protests and pray-ins and planned acts of civil disobedience—as well as teach-ins, rallies, and religious sermons.[139] The work called renewed attention to the plight of the poor—including a two-hour congressional hearing that listened explicitly to the group's demands.[140]

There's a lot that is remarkable about the renewed Poor People's Campaign—not least of which is examining the way the movement takes advantage of everyone's natural abilities. And it rarely requires anything more than time, effort, and a willingness to give of yourself to something greater than yourself.

For example, the way Reverend Barber and Reverend Theoharis lead the campaign is explicitly religious, in part because they are taking advantage of a community they already have: their churches. Instead of running away from that, they lean into it. They use the tools at their disposal—praying and sermonizing and singing—to accomplish their ends.

They are doing the work of bringing us closer to justice—and given the nature of their campaign, no one needs to give a cent to make it happen.

One person who has supported the new Poor People's Campaign was also a key advisor in the old campaign: the singer and social activist Harry Belafonte.[141] It was to Belafonte that Dr. Martin Luther King Jr. confided, during the final days of his life in the tumultuous and violent year of 1968, that he feared America was "a burning house." "I guess," Dr. King said then, "we're just going to become the firemen."[142]

It is my belief that today, more than ever, we each must take it upon ourselves to become the firefighters for justice.

Regardless of wealth, we have it within our power to douse the flames that threaten not one house or another, but all our communities and cities, our countries and continents. We must use the most effective retardant there is—hope—and take advantage of our natural inclinations to come to where help is needed, and to give it with faith and without fear.

But not only that.

We must not only be firefighters. We must be whatever we are—doctors and nurses, pilots and police officers, technologists and teachers—all for justice. Farmers and field hands for justice. Artists and activists for justice. Whoever you are, whatever you do—add two words to your title: "for justice." Do what you do for justice.

> In many ways, we do philanthropy an injustice, for want of another word, when we look at philanthropy as a money thing. The greatest philanthropists aren't doing it with money. They're just living it out.
>
> —STRIVE MASIYIWA, FOUNDER AND CHAIRMAN OF ECONET WIRELESS GROUP

In other words, be a philanthropist. Be a lover of humanity—in the tradition of our New Gospel of Wealth. Take your platform and privileges and talents, and mindfully, with great love and care, aim them toward a more just world.

CONCLUSION

The Tenets of a New Gospel

Every journey needs a guide—and the journey toward justice is no exception. As we perform the good works of this New Gospel of Wealth, the best way to practice what we preach is to follow the tenets we've explored on our journey. We must try to remember to:

- Recognize the privilege of perspective by seeing and sharing access and opportunity;

- Adopt the awareness of ignorance by learning what we don't know;

- Take ownership of selflessness by giving with humility;

- Work to raise the roots by addressing causes, not consequences;

- Harness the power of proximity by valuing both expertise and experience;

- Exercise the courage of conviction by standing up and speaking out; and

- Promote the democracy of justice by recognizing that our liberation is bound together.

Depending on your position, some of these tenets may prove more applicable to you than others. But as times and fashions change, the principles found in this book can remain a constant touchstone in your work.

Of course, these tenets—each in its own way—answer the same fundamental question: *How can we move our work along the continuum from generosity to justice?*

What this book doesn't answer—and what so many people ask when they are starting out—is a different question: *What should my philanthropy look like? And how do I do it?*

Much as there is a spectrum from generosity to justice in terms of what to fund, so too is there a spectrum of actions, tools, and methods for philanthropy that are worth considering.

One approach that has been popular in some corners of philanthropy is known as the "moonshot" project—a big project that is an exciting, ambitious bet with enormous potential. Today's new philanthropists are often intent on finding these kinds of moonshot solutions to problems. They expect to match the genius of their innovations in the private sector with silver-bullet solutions at rocket-ship scale.

This is an admirable goal. After all, a moonshot solution might address the root causes of the problems we seek to address. But attempts at a moonshot often fall short because this approach doesn't go deep enough to have lasting impact.

If the moonshot represents one extreme of the philanthropic spectrum for what you can build—a single massive project—then the other end of the spectrum might be deemed "perpetuity." The

Rockefeller Foundation and the Ford Foundation, for example, are endowed to exist in perpetuity—which has allowed us to continue doing the important work we do for generations past and generations yet to come.

It might be tempting to think that these are the only models. However, other notable philanthropists have created a "sunset date" for their institution, so that all of their funds go to good use as soon as possible. One of my heroes is the philanthropist Julius Rosenwald, a contemporary of Carnegie's who made his fortune as a leader of Sears, Roebuck and Company—the country's largest retailer at the time.[143] After befriending Booker T. Washington, Rosenwald created the Rosenwald Fund, which built more than 5,000 schools in the rural South for black children. Rosenwald asked that the fund be spent in its entirety by 1948. By then, the success of the project was clear. At one point, about one in every three black children in the South were attending a Rosenwald School—including the likes of Maya Angelou and Representative John Lewis.[144] So, although the fund no longer exists, without a doubt we are still experiencing the impact of Rosenwald's philanthropy today.

Another way to ensure longevity, without actually endowing your money for perpetuity, is to build lasting partnerships. Carnegie was a pioneer of this matching grant model, with his famous Carnegie Libraries. Carnegie knew he wanted to build libraries around the world—and with his funds, he could have done it by himself. Instead, he developed what became known as "The Carnegie Formula": Any local government that wanted a library had to first, freely donate the land, and second, commit to spending an amount equal to at least 10 percent of Carnegie's initial grant, every year, to maintain the library.[145]

The result: More than 2,800 libraries were built around the world.[146] And many of them exist to this day.[147]

Without realizing it, Carnegie had created a model for what we now call a public-private partnership. By getting the local government involved and invested, Carnegie ensured that the local community had a stake in the library moving forward, long after the building was finished and his money had gone away.

At the same time, this all assumes we build something new. In fact, for any given problem, there's likely to be an ecosystem of nonprofit organizations and individuals already working to address it. These organizations have learned lessons you didn't know you needed to learn, have more intimate experience with the subject, and are prepared to make a more immediate impact. Rather than creating initiatives from scratch or building up new organizations that will compete with each other for limited funding, it might be more effective to identify existing partners and contribute to their ongoing work.

At the Ford Foundation, we often talk about the three I's: ideas, individuals, and institutions. All three are critical to success. We have found a balance supporting the institutions that will do the slow and necessary work of social change across generations, while also funding the individuals and their ideas, from moonshots to microfinance and more. This work has gone through countless evolutions over the decades, and continues to adapt with changes in the world.

Ultimately, we know there is more than one way to achieve justice. We know that no one person has all the answers. Yet one of the great challenges of this work is how what we can see—and what we can imagine for our work—is limited by our personal story or position in society.

When it comes to the question of what we should fund, the challenge is not new. Carnegie himself believed he could list the top ways philanthropists could use their money. And he did so, in the lesser-known second half of "The Gospel of Wealth," an essay he titled "The Best Fields for Philanthropy." They were, in order of most desirable to least: founding a university, establishing free libraries, supporting hospitals and "other institutions connected with the alleviation of human suffering," providing public parks, providing public baths, and creating and subsidizing churches.[148]

It is a remarkable list.

In contrast, this book does not answer the question of where one should donate one's time or resources. It does not prescribe the causes one ought to support, the methods one ought to use, the projects one ought to fund. Intentionally so.

In part, that's because my "The Best Fields for Philanthropy" might look very different from Carnegie's. But more importantly, your list would likely look different from mine. And that's okay. After all, Carnegie's list is worth considering today not because of what has changed, but because of what all his examples have in common: They are almost all institutions Carnegie himself benefited from.

We know this because Carnegie tells us so. When he describes each field, he explains how it benefited him or people like him. He describes how he personally benefited from access to books at a young age. He emphasizes that "only those who have passed through a lingering and dangerous illness can rate at their true value the care, skill, and attendance of trained female nurses."[149] And from his days in poverty, Carnegie understands that public parks and baths can offer a real service too, offering a keen awareness by quoting the scripture that says "man does not live on bread alone."[150]

Our experiences shape our perspective: what we think is valuable, where we feel inclined to give back or pay it forward. It's the reason universities (the first field on Carnegie's list) enjoy massive donations—including funds for new buildings—from alumni, even as their neighboring and surrounding towns and cities see shortages of affordable housing.

When we think of programs that benefit us, we see them in an individual context, and too often we ignore the larger context and root causes. It seems implicit in "The Gospel of Wealth" that those fortunate enough to live in better circumstances also have better judgment—a kind of self-righteous trap that conflates the value of wealth with the value of an opinion.

But the question is not whether libraries are effective—because they can be and have been for many individuals and communities, myself included. The real question should be whether these interventions are sufficient—especially if the goal is justice and systemic change. This book cannot answer the question of what you should give your money or time to. But I hope when you do decide, you pause to ask: *Why is* this *the thing I have chosen to support? What personal preference or bias am I bringing to this decision?*

Ask yourself: *What might I be overlooking? How can I learn more?*

This is, perhaps, one of the biggest differences between the old Gospel of Wealth and the new one. Carnegie believed that, by virtue of his success, he was best suited to pick the fields for his philanthropy—and that his fleet of experts were the best people to implement it. But today, we know that no one has all the answers. And we know it is vitally important to consult not just experts, but also people who experience the realities we hope to change.

If life treats you well and puts you in a position to give back, then you are, by nature of that position, often less able to judge where and how justice can best be served. After all, you are probably distanced from the problem. You no longer experience certain kinds of inequality as a daily obstacle. You no longer see how injustice manifests itself.

Instead, we must recognize that there is more to life than our daily experience. We must recognize that we are not individual actors—no matter how much we think we are unique. Rather, the struggle to do good is one of the oldest and most noble callings in the history of mankind. When we take up its mantle, we are joining a journey that has preceded us by centuries, and that will continue long after we are gone. Our job is to help steer that path in the right direction—and to recognize that the best way to do so is to listen, learn, and do what we can to demand justice.

Since joining the Ford Foundation, I have been on my own journey for justice—sometimes quite literally. Everywhere I visit, I try to bring something back: an artifact, a memento, or even just an idea. Two of the most important ideas I have collected are represented by two sticky notes, affixed to my computer monitor, on which are written a pair of personal mottos: One says, "Pressure is a privilege." The other says, "You rest, you rust."

These two concepts have guided my thinking time and time again. Whenever I feel stressed, I remind myself that most of the pressures of my life stem from the great privilege I have of steering this noble organization—that such pressures are, in many ways, incomparable to the daily indignities of those our organization aims to serve. And similarly, when I am feeling tired—when I don't wish to challenge convention, and I hope to take the easier path of doing what has always been done—the second sticky reminds me that the challenge of change is always worth it.

As you end your journey with this book, I encourage you to reflect on those two ideas, and consider how the work of justice demands their convergence. Take stock of your own privilege and special skills, and ask how you might press them into service and share them. How might you use what you have to fuel the engine of change?

I also have a suggestion for the phrasing of a commemorative sticky note of your own, one that says simply: "Justice is calling."

It doesn't matter whether you're a college senior vacillating between career possibilities, a computer programmer living in Silicon Valley, or the president of a foundation. This fight implicates you too. It doesn't ever discriminate based on age, status, background, or income level—it's an equal opportunity employer. Each and every one of us can accept its offer of employment, and work to deliver justice to communities that have gone without it for far too long.

Justice is calling. And it's my job. It's *our* job.

Of course, answering that call is no easy feat. One person who understood that was Reverend Dr. Martin Luther King Jr. Over a half century ago, during the final days his life, Dr. King penned what he called "a testament of hope," an epistle he could not have known would be among his last. "Whenever I am asked my opinion of the current state of the civil rights movement," King began, "I am forced to pause; it is not easy to describe a crisis so profound that it has caused the most powerful nation in the world to stagger in confusion and bewilderment."[151]

In the long and sprawling meditation on the state of the world that follows, King offers a template for how he thought about the pursuit of justice. He discusses the privileges that white people do not even realize they have, and the ignorance and bias that is pervasive, even among so-called liberals. He argues that some of the hard-won results of grassroots pressure and organizing—from school integration to the 1964 Civil Rights Act—were being used to bolster the egos and images of politicians and presidents.

What's more, through example after example, he shows how even the toothless parts of these efforts were not being enforced in a way that got at the roots of the problem. This lack of progress, he thought, was in part because most white people could never understand daily racism. They were too far removed from the average black person's life.

In the final paragraphs of the essay, he insists that even a small minority of protesters can be brave and cause dissent—and how, united, "this dissent is America's hope." King finishes by reminding his readers that "Jesus of Nazareth wrote no books; he owned no property to endow him with influence . . . But he changed the course of mankind."[152]

Today, it is encouraging to see that the path King follows in his argument—from understanding privilege to confronting ignorance and bias; putting equality over ego and choosing solutions that take on root causes; getting proximate to the problems and having the moral courage to defend the answers; and recognizing that none of this requires money, just energy—still leads us toward righteousness.

To do all this is a tremendous amount of work. And it would be naïve to assume that most, or even many, will undertake it. There are plenty of reasons to doubt the success of our project. One need only look around to see how much is done wrong, even by those who wish to do right.

Dr. King had a response for this too. In his testament of hope, he wrote that "man has the capacity to do right as well as wrong, and his history is a path upward, not downward . . . This is why I remain an optimist."[153]

So, too, must it be with us. Let us be righteous optimists as we stand before unprecedented challenges. Let us continue to make our way upward. And let us do everything we can to bend the moral arc of the universe toward the better end.

CONTRIBUTORS

ELIZABETH ALEXANDER

Elizabeth Alexander—poet, educator, memoirist, and scholar—is president of the Mellon Foundation, the nation's largest funder of the arts, culture, and humanities. With more than two decades of experience leading innovative programs in education, philanthropy, and beyond, Dr. Alexander has held distinguished professorships at Smith College, Columbia University, and Yale University, and previously served as the director of creativity and free expression at the Ford Foundation. She is chancellor emeritus of the Academy of American Poets and a member of the American Academy of Arts and Sciences, and she serves on the Pulitzer Prize Board. Dr. Alexander composed and delivered "Praise Song for the Day" for the 2009 inauguration of President Barack Obama, and is author or co-author of fifteen books. Her book of poems, *American Sublime*, and her memoir, *The Light of the World*, were finalists for the Pulitzer Prize. Her latest book, released in 2022, is *The Trayvon Generation*.

IKAL ANGELEI

Ikal Angelei is the founder of Friends of Lake Turkana, a grassroots organization dedicated to pushing for social, economic, and environmental justice in Kenya's greater Turkana Basin.

A renowned environmental and human rights activist, Angelei was awarded the Goldman Environmental Prize in 2012 for her work organizing governments, banks, and the Turkana Basin community against the construction of the Gilgel Gibe III Dam, successfully persuading major banks to pull their financial considerations from the project.

Raised in the largely remote and historically marginalized Turkana County in Kenya, Angelei grew up with a strong sense of justice. Even as a young girl, she knew that she would spend her life fighting for her community.

LAURA AND JOHN ARNOLD

Laura and John Arnold are the co-founders and co-chairs of Arnold Ventures, a philanthropy focused on maximizing opportunity and minimizing injustice.

The Arnolds have invested more than $2.5 billion in the research, data, and advocacy needed to uncover the root causes of societal problems and advance effective solutions, with a focus on health care, education, criminal justice, democracy, and public finance.

Both Laura and John are engaged full time in running the organization's operations and charting its long-term vision. John previously worked as an investor and Laura as an attorney and energy executive. They have three children and reside in Houston, Texas.

LAURA ARRILLAGA-ANDREESSEN

Laura Arrillaga-Andreessen is the founder and president of the Laura Arrillaga-Andreessen Foundation (LAAF.org).

Arrillaga-Andreessen founded LAAF.org to provide people of all backgrounds with the necessary resources to make meaningful contributions to philanthropy. Today, the foundation uses technology to globally scale philanthropy education and to advance the philanthropic field through free resources and programs.

A trailblazer in philanthropy education, Arrillaga-Andreessen taught the first-ever grant-making course at Stanford University and the first course on strategic philanthropy at the Stanford Graduate School of Business. She also has developed and teaches the course "Power of You: Women & Leadership" to prepare young women to surmount workplace challenges and to learn to use their positions, roles, voices, and platforms to more intentionally promote inclusivity and social impact.

Arrillaga-Andreessen lives with her husband, technology entrepreneur and venture capitalist Marc Andreessen; their three-year-old son; and two vivacious garden snails named Phillipe and Augustine.

CONNIE BALLMER

Connie Ballmer is the co-founder of Ballmer Group and spouse of Steve Ballmer. Ballmer Group is committed to improving economic mobility for children and families in the United States, funding leaders and organizations that have demonstrated the ability to reshape opportunity and reduce systemic inequities.

Connie's long-standing philanthropic focus has been on the well-being of children, especially those in the foster care system. Connie is a general partner and founding investor at Blue Meridian Partners, a funding collaborative that supports scalable solutions to the problems that limit economic and social mobility. She also serves on the boards of the Obama Foundation and StriveTogether.

An Oregon native, Connie served as a founding member of the governing board at the University of Oregon, where she earned her bachelor's degree, and was inducted into the School of Journalism's Hall of Achievement. Connie and Steve have three sons and reside in Bellevue, Washington.

STEVE BALLMER

Steve Ballmer is the co-founder of Ballmer Group and spouse of Connie Ballmer. Ballmer Group is committed to improving economic mobility for children and families in the United States, funding leaders and organizations that have demonstrated the ability to reshape opportunity and reduce systemic inequities.

Steve is the former CEO of Microsoft. During his tenure, the company grew to almost $80 billion in revenue and became the third most profitable company in the United States. He is also the chairman of the Los Angeles Clippers basketball team and the founder of USAFacts, a nonprofit seeking to ground our public debates in fact and to improve transparency in government. He has taught numerous courses at Stanford University.

Steve grew up near Detroit, where his father worked as a manager at Ford Motor Company. Steve and Connie have three sons and reside in Bellevue, Washington.

KEN FRAZIER

Kenneth C. Frazier is executive chairman of the board at Merck, a role he began in July 2021, following his retirement from a decade-long tenure as Merck's president and CEO.

Prior to joining Merck in 1992, Frazier was a partner with Drinker Biddle & Reath. He sits on several boards and is co-founder/co-chair of OneTen, a coalition committed to upskilling, hiring, and promoting one million Black Americans into family-sustaining jobs. Frazier is chairman of health assurance initiatives at General Catalyst and co-chair of legal services at Corporation's Leaders Council.

As a strong advocate for social justice and economic inclusion, Frazier is the recipient of numerous awards and honors, especially in the legal, business, and humanitarian fields. Frazier was named one of the World's Greatest Leaders by *Fortune* magazine and was also named one of *TIME*'s 100 Most Influential People, twice. He became the first recipient of the Forbes Lifetime Achievement Award for Healthcare, and his peers named Frazier *Chief Executive* magazine's CEO of the Year.

NICK HANAUER

Nick Hanauer is the co-founder of the venture capital firm Second Avenue Partners and the founder of Civic Ventures, an organization devoted to driving social change.

. In addition to being an accomplished entrepreneur, Hanauer is a national leader on policy issues such as raising the minimum wage and preventing gun violence. As a dedicated proponent of public education, Hanauer co-founded the nonpartisan League of Education Voters in Washington. He also serves as board member to numerous organizations such as the Cascade Land Conservancy and the University of Washington Foundation. Hanauer has written two books—*The True Patriot* and *The Gardens of Democracy*—with co-author Eric Liu and serves as a board advisor to the journal *Democracy*.

Hanauer and his wife, Leslie, believe deeply in the power of philanthropy. Keeping with their commitment to public education and the environment, the Hanauers run the Nick and Leslie Hanauer Foundation. Together, they have signed the Giving Pledge, committing themselves to donating more than half of their fortune to philanthropic causes.

CARLY HARE

Carly Hare (Pawnee/Yankton) is committed to advancing equity and community engagement. She is a proud mother, daughter, sister, auntie, partner, ally, and friend. Her Pawnee name is <i kita u hoo <i]a hiks, "kind leader of men."

Hare currently serves as the first executive director of Culture Surge. Previously, Hare served as the national director of CHANGE Philanthropy and led Native Americans in

Philanthropy. Hare also held the positions of director of development for the Native American Rights Fund and director of programs for Community Foundation Boulder County.

Hare chaired the Colorado Independent Congressional Redistricting Commission, the Highlander Center, and the Impact on Education boards. She is on the advisory committee for the Boulder County Marshall Fire Recovery Fund and the Women & Girls of Color Fund at the Women's Foundation of Colorado.

Carly Hare is known for balancing grace with grit, and filling a room with her generous laugh and powerful *lulu*.

MELLODY HOBSON

Mellody Hobson is co-CEO and president of Ariel Investments, LLC, and chairman of the company's publicly traded mutual funds. She is also co-founder of Ariel Alternatives, LLC, the firm's private equity subsidiary.

Additionally, she is chair of Starbucks Corporation and a director of JPMorgan Chase. She previously served as chairman of DreamWorks Animation and was a long-standing board member of the Estée Lauder Companies. Hobson is vice chair of World Business Chicago, co-chair of the Lucas Museum of Narrative Art, and a board member of the George Lucas Education Foundation and Bloomberg Philanthropies. She also serves on the boards of the Los Angeles County Museum of Art (LACMA), the Rockefeller Foundation, and the executive committee of the Investment Company Institute.

Hobson earned her AB from Princeton University's School of Public and International Affairs.

GEORGE KAISER

George Kaiser is the CEO and primary owner of the parent of Kaiser-Francis Oil Company. He is also the chairman of the board and majority owner of BOK Financial Corporation and a major shareholder in a number of diversified businesses in North America and overseas.

Kaiser is the grantor of the George Kaiser Family Foundation (GKFF), which has the primary mission of providing equal opportunity for young children. GKFF develops and manages programs in early childhood education, social service support, criminal justice interventions and advocacy, civic enhancement projects, and community health initiatives, all under the mantra "No newborn child bears any responsibility for the circumstances of her birth and yet her future chance for success in life is heavily influenced by those circumstances." GKFF's civic ventures are designed to rewrite this paradigm and to add to the diversity, equity, and vibrancy of the Tulsa, Oklahoma, area.

During his life and through his estate, Kaiser plans to contribute his entire net worth to GKFF.

STRIVE MASIYIWA

Strive Masiyiwa is the founder and chairman of the Econet Group, a pan-African telecommunications, media, and technology company with operations and investments in twenty-nine countries.

He serves on several international boards including Unilever, National Geographic Society, and the global advisory boards of the Council on Foreign Relations and Stanford University. A former board member of the Rockefeller Foundation for fifteen years, he also serves as chairman of the Alliance for a Green Revolution in Africa (AGRA). He previously served on the Africa Progress Panel and as a juror on the Hilton Humanitarian Prize.

As a philanthropist, Masiyiwa is a member of the Giving Pledge and his contributions to education, health, and development have been widely recognized. Masiyiwa and his wife finance the Higherlife Foundation, which has supported the education of over 250,000 African children over the past twenty years.

Over the last few years, Masiyiwa has devoted his time to mentoring the next generation of African entrepreneurs through his Facebook page, which has a growing following of nearly four million young people from across the continent. For over two years, Facebook has identified his platform as having the most engaged following of any business leader in the world.

AI-JEN POO

Ai-jen Poo serves as the president of the National Domestic Workers Alliance and the executive director of Caring Across Generations.

Poo is a leading voice in the future of work and the future of care for families. She played a crucial role in New York's adoption of the Domestic Workers Bill of Rights, which quickly became a national standard. Her work has catalyzed a growing demand to invest in care as essential infrastructure. Fighting for the rights of women, caregivers, immigrants, and domestic workers, Poo's work is a part of many social movements to address inequality and strengthen our economy and democracy.

Poo has served as a featured speaker at the Aspen Ideas Festival, TED Women, the Milken Institute, and the White House

Conference on Aging. She is also the author of *The Age of Dignity: Preparing for the Elder Boom in a Changing America*.

Poo is a 2014 MacArthur Fellow, a *TIME* 100 alumna, a commissioner on President Biden's Asian American Native Hawaiian and Pacific Islander Commission, and a member of the Ford Foundation Board of Trustees.

LAURENE POWELL JOBS

Laurene Powell Jobs is founder and president of Emerson Collective. Using philanthropy, investments, arts and culture, and convening, Emerson Collective creates opportunities and builds solutions to inspire lasting change in education, the environment, immigration, and health equity. Powell Jobs's commitment to renewing America's calcified social systems deepened over two decades ago with her work in education.

In 1997, she founded College Track, a college completion program where she remains board chair, to address the alarming opportunity and achievement gaps among students. She is also co-founder and board chair of the XQ Institute, the nation's leading organization dedicated to transforming the American high school. In keeping with her belief in supporting journalism as a vital civic institution, Powell Jobs is owner and board chair of *The Atlantic*. Powell Jobs also serves on the boards of Chicago CRED, the Council on Foreign Relations, the Ford Foundation, and Elemental Excelerator, where she is board chair. In addition, she is a member of the National Academy of Arts and Sciences, and a recipient of the Stanford Graduate School of Business Ernest C. Arbuckle Award for managerial excellence and addressing the changing needs of society.

JEFF RAIKES

Jeff Raikes is co-founder of the Raikes Foundation with his wife, Tricia. Through this work, they noticed patterns in how systems treated people differently based on their identity, perpetuating unequal and unfair outcomes based on race—or racialized outcomes. They want to do their part to make these systems work for everyone and ensure that, in America, everyone matters and has an opportunity to thrive.

Jeff is the former CEO of the Bill & Melinda Gates Foundation, where he led the foundation's efforts to promote equity for people around the world. Before joining the foundation, Jeff was president of Microsoft's Business Division and served as a member of the company's senior leadership team that set the overall strategy and direction for the firm.

Currently, he is part of the ownership group of the Seattle Mariners and serves on its board. He also serves on the board of Costco Wholesale Corporation, the Raikes School at the University of Nebraska-Lincoln, Green Diamond Resource Company, and Hudl. After ten years of board service, Jeff is a Chair Emeritus at Stanford University.

TRICIA RAIKES

Tricia Raikes is a philanthropist, advocate, and executive who collaborates with communities, government, and business leaders to advance racial justice and equity in our country. Tricia believes that progress on our most enduring challenges requires investing in leaders with lived expertise, strong field experience, and strategic advocacy.

Tricia is the co-founder of the Raikes Foundation with her husband, Jeff. Inspired by the values they were raised with, their foundation focuses on transforming youth-serving systems to be more equitable and accessible so that all young people can achieve healthy life outcomes and increased agency. Tricia's background is in marketing communications, and she previously led Creative Services at Microsoft.

A longtime advocate for research universities, Tricia serves on the advisory boards for Stanford's Graduate School of Education, Stanford's Undergraduate Cabinet, and the Raikes School of Computer Science and Management at the University of Nebraska. She is also part of the ownership group of the Seattle Mariners.

Tricia was recognized as a White House Champion of Change by President Obama for her work to prevent and end youth homelessness.

DAVID ROCKEFELLER JR.

David Rockefeller Jr. serves as a board member of Rockefeller Capital Management, a trustee of the Rockefeller Brothers Fund, and a member of the Council on Foreign Relations.

As a prominent business leader and lifelong philanthropist, Rockefeller has been a longtime supporter of the arts, education, and environmental conservation. He has served as a trustee of the Asian Cultural Council, a trustee of the Museum of Modern Art, a fellow of the American Academy of Arts and Sciences, and a citizen chair of the National Parks Foundation.

In 2004, Rockefeller merged his passion for sailing with his commitment to environmental preservation by founding Sailors for the Sea—a nonprofit dedicated to protecting the oceans—which is now a program of Oceana.

DAVID SKORTON

David Skorton, MD, is president and CEO of the Association of American Medical Colleges (AAMC), which represents the nation's medical schools, teaching hospitals, health systems, and academic societies.

Previously, as secretary of the Smithsonian Institution, he oversaw nineteen museums, twenty-one libraries, the National Zoo, research centers, and education programs. Prior to that, he was president of two universities, Cornell University and the University of Iowa, where he served on the faculty for twenty-six years and specialized in treating adolescents and adults with congenital heart disease.

He is an elected member of the National Academy of Medicine, the American Academy of Arts and Sciences, and the American Philosophical Society, as well as a lifetime member of the Council on Foreign Relations and a fellow of the American Association for the Advancement of Science.

Dr. Skorton earned his BA and MD degrees from Northwestern University. He completed his medical residency and fellowship in cardiology and was chief medical resident at the University of California, Los Angeles.

JON STRYKER

Jon Stryker is the founder and board president of the Arcus Foundation, a nonprofit designed to advocate for LGBTQ human rights and for the protection of the world's gibbons and great apes. Since its founding, the Arcus Foundation has contributed more than $600 million to both LGBTQ and conservation causes around the world. From 2006 to 2012, Stryker held a spot as one of *The Chronicle of Philanthropy*'s top 50 donors in the nation.

Stryker is a founding board member of the Ol Pejeta Conservancy in Kenya and of Save the Chimps, the world's largest chimpanzee sanctuary. In 2017, he was named a Patron of Nature by the International Union for Conservation of Nature.

Originally from Kalamazoo, Michigan, Stryker now resides in New York City.

LAURIE TISCH

Laurie M. Tisch is founder and president of the Laurie M. Tisch Illumination Fund, dedicated to increasing access and opportunity for all New Yorkers and fostering healthy and vibrant communities. Since its inception in 2007, the Illumination Fund has undertaken high-impact initiatives, including Healthy Food & Community Change, launched in 2013, and Arts in Health, launched in 2018. The fund has played a catalytic role in a range of initiatives and organizations, as well as engaging in public-private partnerships with multiple city agencies.

She is secretary and former co-chair of the board of trustees at the Whitney Museum of American Art and is vice chair of the board of trustees at Lincoln Center for the Performing Arts. She serves on the boards of the Aspen Institute, the Juilliard School, and the Jewish Communal Fund, and is chair emeritus of the Center for Arts Education and the Children's Museum of Manhattan (CMOM).

ALICE WALTON

Alice Walton is a philanthropist and the founder of the Alice L. Walton Foundation, Alice L. Walton School of Medicine, Art Bridges Foundation, Crystal Bridges Museum of American Art, and the Whole Health Institute.

Walton has long been committed to increasing access to art in communities across the country. To advance this aim, she has served as a board member of the Amon Carter Museum in Fort Worth, Texas, the trustees' council of the National Gallery of Art in Washington, D.C., and the advisory council of the Smithsonian American Women's History Museum.

For her dedicated and exemplary work in the field, Walton has received the Smithsonian Institution's Archives of American Art Medal and the Getty Medal for contributions to the Arts and Humanities. Walton was recognized in 2012 as one of the most influential people in the world by *TIME* magazine and in 2018 was inducted into the International Women's Forum Hall of Fame.

ACKNOWLEDGMENTS

When I reflect on my decades-long journey with, in, and through philanthropy, I am humbled by how much I owe to so many. I would not have made it this far without the support of countless mentors, teachers, colleagues, champions, and friends—but for now, I will limit my expressions of gratitude to a smaller group that has made this book, and all it represents, possible.

My first foray into philanthropy came at the Children's Storefront School in Harlem when I joined the board in 1989 and learned countless lessons from Ned O'Gorman and Elsie V. Aidinoff. Through the Storefront I was introduced to the late Calvin Butts, the brilliant and charismatic pastor of the Abyssinian Baptist Church, and the dynamic Karen Phillips, who hired me in the early days of the Abyssinian Development Corporation. Working from a tiny basement office on West 138th Street I was afforded a remarkable opportunity to live in Harlem and play a part in the revitalization of that historic community.

During my time at Abyssinian, I was first exposed to some exemplary foundation program staff. Thank you, Mary Jo Mullan, Hildy Simmons, Nancy Roob, and Karen Rosa for modeling patience, care, and rigor when I was your grantee, and for treating our organization with trust and respect. I have to also acknowledge Sharon King, a great mentor whose death left a hole in my heart.

It has deeply informed my journey in philanthropy and the way we serve our partners and colleagues at the Ford Foundation today.

Serving as director of the US program at the Rockefeller Foundation was an enormous honor. For that, thank you, Julia Lopez and Sir Gordon Conway, for taking a risk and hiring me when I had little knowledge of philanthropy, even less experience, and despite a few insiders cautioning that I "wasn't Rockefeller Foundation material." At Rockefeller, it was Judith Rodin who promoted me to vice president and taught me invaluable lessons on leadership. I was privileged to work with and learn from the global community's best in health and agriculture, resilience and innovation, urban planning and global development.

Long before I came to the Ford Foundation, I revered the legendary Franklin Thomas as one of the great leaders of the twentieth century. And now, as president, I owe Frank a tremendous debt of gratitude for taking a foundation that was on the brink of insolvency after years of overspending and bad financial markets, and resetting the organization for impact, financial security, and long-term growth. Frank provided me with unwavering mentorship and support for well over a decade, and his perspicacious voice still echoes in the halls of the Ford Foundation and across philanthropy.

I'm indebted to Susan Berresford, who left a powerful legacy and whose counsel I still rely on. Many thanks to my predecessor Luis Ubiñas, who convinced me to leave the Rockefeller Foundation and join the leadership team at Ford. As president, I have benefited beyond measure from the wisdom, counsel, and support of the best board of trustees in philanthropy—full stop. And I have been particularly blessed by a succession of three extraordinary Chairs of the Board of Trustees: Irene Hirano Inouye, Kofi Appenteng, and now Francisco G. Cigarroa.

Along with the Ford Foundation's board, my colleagues at the foundation challenge and sustain me on a daily basis. Our leadership team—Martín Abregú, Depelsha McGruder, Sarita Gupta, Nishka Chandrasoma, Eric Doppstadt, Michele Moore, Hilary Pennington, and Diane Samuels—have been absolutely integral in steering this great foundation and the field of philanthropy toward justice.

In the fall of 2015, I wrote a letter and then a *New York Times* op-ed, outlining a New Gospel of Wealth, drawing inspiration from many sources, but especially Andrew Carnegie's original "The Gospel of Wealth," Dr. Martin Luther King Jr.'s insights on the inequalities that make philanthropy both possible and necessary, and Anand Giridharadas's provocative distinction between generosity and justice. The New Gospel became a means for convening some of the most important voices in philanthropy. In the years since, many of them have joined me in considering a vital question: If there is a continuum between generosity and justice, how do we push our work closer to the latter?

The New Gospel of Wealth project was executed by our hard-working Office of Communications—led by Michele Moore and her dedicated team. You have succeeded—and exceeded—in your mission to amplify this message beyond our walls, and our entire sector is better for it.

I am thankful to Jonas Kieffer and his talented team at West Wing Writers for your strategic partnership in producing these pages and so many others over so many years. And a very eager thank you to Kris Pauls and Disruption Books for shepherding me through all of the twists and turns of the publication process, and for creating such a gorgeous book, inside and out.

Of course, I would never get anywhere without the diligent and fearless colleagues who manage my whirlwind life, led by my chief of staff Taara Rangarajan. Your rare combination of organizational prowess and optimistic attitude—not to mention good humor—make it possible for me to fly through even my most action-packed days.

Then, there are friends outside the foundation who went above and beyond to bring this book to life, and helped shape my thinking and career.

Laura Arrillaga-Andreessen: You have expanded the definition of philanthropy and are serving a new generation of givers and leaders at Stanford. You are a terrific partner and an even better friend.

To the unofficial dean of philanthropy, Professor Joel Fleishman: I am grateful for years and years of mentorship and counsel, for me and for all of the academics and scholars working to think through the history and future of giving.

Agnes Gund: Without your singular vision and humble leadership, there would be no Art for Justice. Your insight into the connection between creativity and social justice is one that I hope spreads far and wide.

Laurene Powell Jobs: You are a force for good, representing a new generation of philanthropists, innovating and modeling new and different ways of bringing justice to all. I am thankful to have you as both a beacon for the future of philanthropy and as a dear friend.

Jon Stryker: Thank you for affording me the privilege of supporting you on your journey to create the Arcus Foundation. From that vantage point, I learned so much about the challenges of creating a private foundation from early stage to maturity—and how to approach those challenges with humility and humanity.

Joan Ganz Cooney and Holly Peterson: You are the most dynamic mother-daughter team in philanthropy. Your impact on children's issues and criminal justice reform is immeasurable. I treasure our friendship.

Jim Canales, Mark Malloch-Brown, Patti Harris, Alberto Ibargüen, Larry Kramer, Rip Rapson, Bob Ross, Raj Shah, John Palfrey, Sam Gill, Mark Suzman, and La June Montgomery Tabron: I have treasured working closely with you and all that you continue to teach me.

I am energized by the giving of Melinda Gates and MacKenzie Scott, two women who have demonstrated the power of principled and courageous philanthropy that centers people closest to the problems—especially women and girls—in their grant-making and advocacy.

I think often of the giants—mentors and friends—who have passed during the last several years, among them Vartan Gregorian, Vernon Jordan, and, of course, Franklin Thomas. I am lucky to stand on their shoulders still.

Finally, I extend my eternal gratitude and thanks toward all of the advocates, thought leaders, and drum majors for justice who agreed to speak to me for this book. *From Generosity to Justice: A New Gospel of Wealth* is as much yours as it is mine. Your insights and insistence, conversations and confrontations are not just central to the book; they *are* the book. I am, as always, grateful for your vision and voice, honored to strive, and struggle, and serve alongside you, and optimistic—*radically* optimistic—that, together, we will move our world closer to justice.

NOTES

1 "The Gilded Age," PBS, http://www.pbs.org/wgbh/americanexperience/
features/carnegie-gilded/.

2 Lily Rothman, "How American Inequality in the Gilded Age Compares to Today,"
TIME, February 5, 2018, http://time.com/5122375/american
-inequality-gilded-age/.

3 Chuck Collins and Josh Hoxie, "Billionaire Bonanza," Inequality.org, November
2017, https://inequality.org/wp-content/uploads/2017/11/BILLIONAIRE
-BONANZA-2017-Embargoed.pdf.

4 Larry Elliott, "World's 26 richest people own as much as poorest 50%, says
Oxfam," *Guardian*, January 20, 2019, https://www.theguardian.com/
business/2019/jan/21/world-26-richest-people-own-as-much-as-poorest-50
-per-cent-oxfam-report.

5 Rupert Neate, "World's witnessing a new Gilded Age as billionaires' wealth
swells to $6tn," *Guardian*, October 26, 2017, https://www.theguardian.com/
business/2017/oct/26/worlds-witnessing-a-new-gilded-age-as-billionaires-
wealth-swells-to-6tn, Mark Price and Estelle Sommeiller, "The New Gilded
Age? It's Everywhere," *The American Prospect*, August 14, 2018, http://
prospect.org/article/new-gilded-age-its-everywhere, Susan B. Glasser, "The
New Gilded Age," *POLITICO*, July/August 2014, https://www.politico.com/
magazine/story/2014/06/editors-note-108020, Sarah Jones, "Lessons from
the Gilded Age," *The New Republic*, June 13, 2018, https://newrepublic.com/
article/149005/lessons-gilded-age.

6 Andrew Carnegie, "The Gospel of Wealth" (New York: Carnegie Corporation of
New York, 2017), https://www.carnegie.org/media/filer_public/0a/
e1/0ae166c5-fca3-4adf-82a7-74c0534cd8de/gospel_of_wealth_2017.pdf.

7 Nina Martin and Renee Montagne, "U.S. Has the Worst Rate of Maternal
Deaths in the Developed World," NPR, May 12, 2017, https://www.npr.
org/2017/05/12/528098789/u-s-has-the-worst-rate-of-maternal-deaths-in
-the-developed-world.

8 Henry Ford II, "Letter of Resignation," _Philanthropy Roundtable_, March/
April 1977, https://www.philanthropyroundtable.org/home/resources/donor
-intent/donor-intent-resource-library/when-philanthropy-goes-wrong/the
-ford-foundation-and-safe-guarding-donor-intent/letter-of-resignation-by
-henry-ford-ii.

9 "The Power of Help and Hope After Katrina by the Numbers: Volunteers in the Gulf," Corporation for National & Community Service, https://www.nationalservice.gov/pdf/katrina_volunteers_respond.pdf.

10 Ibid.

11 Carl Quintanilla, "Billions in aid given to help Katrina victims," NBC News, August 29, 2006, http://www.nbcnews.com/id/14574567/ns/nbc_nightly_news_with_brian_williams-after_katrina/t/billions-aid-given-help-katrina-victims/#.XIFC5tFOlTZ.

12 Bruce Nolan, "Impoverished women from war-torn Uganda, many of them with HIV, perform arduous labor for weeks to raise nearly $900 for local hurricane victims," Meeting Point International, November 30, 2005, http://meetingpoint-int.org/home/2005/11/30/impoverished-women-from-war-torn-uganda-many-of-them-with-hiv-perform-arduous-labor-for-weeks-to-raise-nearly-900-for-local-hurricane-victims/.

13 Adam B. Kushner, "I'm from New Orleans, and I didn't think we should save it. I was wrong," *Chicago Tribune,* August 29, 2015, http://www.chicagotribune.com/news/opinion/commentary/ct-wapo-new-orleans-rebuild-20150829-story.html.

14 Judith Rodin, "What We've Learned from New Orleans," Rockefeller Foundation, August 24, 2015, https://www.rockefellerfoundation.org/blog/what-the-rockefeller-foundation-has-learned-from-new-orleans/.

15 "Citizen Participation in the Unified New Orleans Plan," Case Study Database, Duke Sanford Center for Strategic Philanthropy and Civil Society, 2007, http://cspcs.sanford.duke.edu/learning-resources/case-study-database/citizen-participation-unified-new-orleans-plan.

16 "The Rockefeller Foundation 2015 Annual Report," The Rockefeller Foundation, 2015, https://www.rockefellerfoundation.org/about-us/governance-reports/annual-reports/annual-report-2015/.

17 "Address by Nelson Mandela for the 'Make Poverty History' Campaign, London—United Kingdom," Speeches by Nelson Mandela, Nelson Rolihlahla Mandela, February 3, 2005, http://www.mandela.gov.za/mandela_speeches/2005/050203_poverty.htm.

18 "Giving Statistics," Charity Navigator, https://www.charitynavigator.org/index.cfm?bay=content.view&cpid=42.

19 Andrew Carnegie, "The Gospel of Wealth."

20 Ibid.

21 Jeremy Deaton, "Hurricane Harvey hit low-income communities hardest," ThinkProgress, September 1, 2017, https://thinkprogress.org/hurricane-harvey-hit-low-income-communities-hardest-6d13506b7e60/.

22 Ibid.

23 "Chimamanda Ngozi Adichie addressed the class of 2015 at Wellesley's
    137th Commencement Exercises," Commencement Address, Wellesley
    College, https://www.wellesley.edu/events/commencement/archives/2015/
    commencementaddress.

24 Francesca Gino and Gary P. Pisano, "Why Leaders Don't Learn from Success,"
    Harvard Business Review, April, 2011, https://hbr.org/2011/04/why-leaders
    -dont-learn-from-success.

25 Peggy McIntosh, "White Privilege and Male Privilege: A Personal Account
    of Coming to See Correspondence Through Work in Women's Studies,"
    National Seed Project, 1988, https://nationalseedproject.org/white-privilege
    -and-male-privilege.

26 Joshua Rothman, "The Origins of 'Privilege,'" *New Yorker,* May 12, 2014,
    https://www.newyorker.com/books/page-turner/the-origins-of-privilege.

27 Ibid.

28 "The Rockefeller Foundation Charter," The Rockefeller Foundation, https://
    assets.rockefellerfoundation.org/app/uploads/20150530122332/Rockefeller
    -Foundation-Charter.pdf.

29 JP Mangalindan, "The secretive billionaire who built Silicon Valley," *Fortune,*
    July 7, 2014, http://fortune.com/2014/07/07/arrillaga-silicon-valley/.

30 "Laura Arrillaga-Andreessen," Biography, Laura Arrillaga-Andreessen
    Foundation, http://www.laaf.org/laura-arrillaga-andreessen.

31 Andrew Carnegie, "The Gospel of Wealth."

32 Laura Spelman Rockefeller, The Rockefellers, Rockefeller Archive Center,
    http://rockarch.org/bio/laura.php.

33 "Spelman College," Education Colleges and Universities, New Georgia
    Encyclopedia, last modified January 2, 2004, http://www.georgiaencyclopedia
    .org/articles/education/spelman-college.

34 "Mellon Mays Undergraduate Fellowship Program," The Andrew W. Mellon
    Foundation, https://mellon.org/programs/diversity/mellon-mays
    -undergraduate-fellowship-program/.

35 Hilary Holladay, "No Ordinary Woman: Lucille Clifton," *Poets & Writers,*
    March 4, 2010, https://www.pw.org/content/no_ordinary_woman_lucille_
    clifton?article_page=2.

36 James Baldwin, "Stranger in the Village," *Notes of a Native Son* (Boston: Beacon
    Press, 1955), http://swc2.hccs.edu/kindle/baldwin.pdf.

37 James Baldwin, *No Name in the Street* (New York City: Dial Press, 1972), 139.

38 Stephanie Eckardt, "With Ava DuVernay's Blessing, Agnes Gund Says Now Is 'the Time' to Reform America's Criminal Justice System," *W Magazine,* https://www.wmagazine.com/story/agnes-gund-interview-mass-incarceration-moma-ps1-gala.

39 Eden King and Kristen Jones, "Why Subtle Bias Is So Often Worse Than Blatant Discrimination," *Harvard Business Review,* https://hbr.org/2016/07/why-subtle-bias-is-so-often-worse-than-blatant-discrimination.

40 "Factsheet on Persons with Disabilities," Resources, United Nations, https://www.un.org/development/desa/disabilities/resources/factsheet-on-persons-with-disabilities.html.

41 "How is poverty status related to disability?" Official Data Breakdown, University of California Davis Center for Poverty Research, https://poverty.ucdavis.edu/faq/how-poverty-status-related-disability.

42 "Persons with a Disability: Labor Force Characteristics," Bureau of Labor Statistics, https://www.bls.gov/news.release/pdf/disabl.pdf.

43 "Educational Attainment in the United States: 2015," United States Census Bureau, https://www.census.gov/content/dam/Census/library/publications/2016/demo/p20-578.pdf.

44 "About Crystal Bridges," Crystal Bridges Museum of American Art, https://crystalbridges.org/about.

45 Carol Ryrie Brink, *Caddie Woodlawn's Family* (New York City: Aladdin Books, 1990), 93.

46 Jim Dwyer, "'James Bond of Philanthropy' Gives Away the Last of His Fortune," *New York Times,* January 5, 2017, https://www.nytimes.com/2017/01/05/nyregion/james-bond-of-philanthropy-gives-away-the-last-of-his-fortune.html.

47 Ibid.

48 "An Entrepreneur Always," The Atlantic Philanthropies, https://www.atlanticphilanthropies.org/chuck-feeneys-story/chapter-1.

49 "Southern African HIV Clinicians Society," Grantees, The Atlantic Philanthropies, https://www.atlanticphilanthropies.org/grantees/southern-african-hiv-clinicians-society.

50 Judith Miller, "He Gave Away $600 Million, and No One Knew," *New York Times,* January 23, 1997, https://www.nytimes.com/1997/01/23/nyregion/he-gave-away-600-million-and-no-one-knew.html.

51 Emily Sanders Hopkins, "The Transformer: Chuck Feeney '56 champions the pleasure of giving while living," *Ezra Cornell's Quarterly Magazine,* Fall 2014, https://ezramagazine.cornell.edu/FALL14/cover.html.

52 "Bloomberg Billionaires Index," Bloomberg, May 2, 2019, https://www.bloomberg.com/billionaires/profiles/jon-l-stryker/.

53 Xaxa (Shasha), "I started Econet with only $75 says Strive Masiyiwa, urges graduates to create jobs instead of looking for them," *Pindula News*, April 6, 2017, https://news.pindula.co.zw/2017/04/06/started-econet-75-says-strive -masiyiwa-urges-graduates-create-jobs-instead-looking/.

54 Mfonobong Nsehe, "Zimbabwe Gets Its First Billionaire," *Forbes*, January 10, 2018, https://www.forbes.com/sites/mfonobongnsehe/2018/01/10/zimbabwe -gets-its-first-billionaire/.

55 "How We Work," Higherlife Foundation, https://www.higherlifefoundation .com/how-we-work/.

56 Ibid.

57 Martin Luther King, Jr., *Strength to Love* (Philadelphia, PA: Fortress, 2010).

58 Pascal Robert, "Ella Baker and the Limits of Charismatic Masculinity," *Huffington Post*, December 6, 2017, https://www.huffingtonpost.com/pascal -robert/ella-baker-and-the-limits_b_2718608.html.

59 Ibid.

60 Ibid.

61 Ibid.

62 Ted Conover, "'Just Mercy,' by Bryan Stevenson," *New York Times*, October 17, 2014, https://www.nytimes.com/2014/10/19/books/review/just-mercy-by -bryan-stevenson.html.

63 Terry Pristin, "Harlem's Pathmark Anchors a Commercial Revival on 125th Street," *New York Times*, November 13, 1999, https://www.nytimes.com/ 1999/11/13/nyregion/harlem-s-pathmark-anchors-a-commercial-revival-on -125th-street.html.

64 Kevin Conley, "Bryan Stevenson Is Working to Transform How Society's Most Vulnerable Access Legal Aid," *Town & Country*, May 2, 2016, https://www .townandcountrymag.com/society/politics/a5602/bryan-stevenson-equal -justice-initiative/.

65 Ibid.

66 Ibid.

67 "The National Memorial for Peace and Justice," Equal Justice Initiative, https:// eji.org/national-lynching-memorial.

68 Ibid.

69 Henry Ford II, "Letter of Resignation by Henry Ford II."

70 Adam Smith, *An Inquiry into the Nature and Causes of the Wealth of Nations* (1776), http://geolib.com/smith.adam/won1-08.html.

71 "The 1969 Private Foundations Law: Historical Perspective on its Origins and Underpinnings," Caplin & Drysdale Attorneys, January 1, 2000, http://www .capdale.com/the-1969-private-foundation-law-historical-perspective-on-its -origins-and-underpinnings.

72 "Nick Hanauer Wants You To Know Everything You Know About Economics Is Wrong," *Forbes*, January 26, 2018, https://www.forbes.com/sites/ robbmandelbaum/2018/01/23/nick-hanauer-wants-you-to-know-everything -you-know-about-economics-is-wrong/#3ffba86564fb.

73 Lynn Thompson, "Seattle City Council approves historic $15 minimum wage," *Seattle Times*, January 25, 2016, https://www.seattletimes.com/seattle-news/ seattle-city-council-approves-historic-15-minimum-wage/.

74 "Wage and Hour Division (WHD)," U.S. Department of Labor, https:// www.dol.gov/whd/state/tipped.htm, "Seattle Minimum Wage," Working Washington, http://www.workingwa.org/seattle-minimum-wage/.

75 Nick Hanauer, "To My Fellow Plutocrats: You Can Cure Trumpism."

76 Ibid.

77 Rikki Renya and Erin Durkin, "Brownsville is Brooklyn's worst neighborhood for children due to high poverty, lousy access to fresh food and day care," *New York Daily News*, March 26, 2017, http://www.nydailynews.com/new-york/ brooklyn/brownsville-brooklyn-worst-neighborhood-children -article-1.3009978.

78 Ibid.

79 Ibid.

80 "Home," The Melting Pot Foundation, https://www.meltingpotfoundationusa .org/.

81 Ibid.

82 Ginia Bellafante, "Brooklyn's Anti-Gentrification Restaurant," *New York Times*, July 27, 2017, https://www.nytimes.com/2017/07/27/nyregion/claus-meyer -brownsville-culinary-center-brooklyn.html.

83 "Home," The Melting Pot Foundation, https://www.meltingpotfoundationusa .org/.

84 "Carly Hare," Council on Foundations, https://www.cof.org/person/carly-hare.

85 "About Common Counsel Foundation," Common Counsel Foundation, https:// www.commoncounsel.org/about/.

86 "Now More Than Ever," D5 Coalition, http://www.d5coalition.org/2016/11/ diversity-equity-and-inclusion-in-philanthropy-what-now/.

87 Carly Hare, "Now is the time to build a movement for philanthropic equity," *Alliance*, December 5, 2017, https://www.alliancemagazine.org/letter/now -time-build-movement-philanthropic-equity/.

88 According to the Indian Land Tenure Foundation: "the 1887 General Allotment Act (or Dawes Act), [was] legislation that was designed to assimilate American Indian people into white culture and was directly responsible for the loss of ninety million acres of Indian land. The Act required tribally-held land to be divided among individual tribal members and the remaining 'surplus' lands opened to white settlement." Source: "Land Issues," ILTF, https://iltf.org/land-issues/issues/.

89 Langston Hughes, "Motto," All Poetry, https://allpoetry.com/poem/8495523-Motto-by-Langston-Hughes.

90 "What is college for," Bard Prison Institute, https://bpi.bard.edu/.

91 William Easterly, *The Tyranny of Experts: Economists, Dictators, and the Forgotten Rights of the Poor* (New York: Basic Books, 2015).

92 Melinda Gates, "From condoms to toilets, why good design is essential for improving global health," *Vox,* May 20, 2015, https://www.vox.com/2015/5/20/8602499/melinda-gates-user-centered-design.

93 Linette Lopez, "The Tisch Dynasty: How Two Boys from Brooklyn Became the Biggest Name in New York," *Business Insider,* May 9, 2012, https://www.businessinsider.com/meet-the-tischs-2012-5.

94 "Our Mission," Who We Are, Laurie M. Tisch Illumination Fund, https://thelmtif.org/who-we-are/our-mission/.

95 "Interview of Ai-jen Poo," Democracy Collaborative, May 2014, https://democracycollaborative.org/content/ai-jen-poo.

96 "About the National Domestic Workers Alliance," National Domestic Workers Alliance, https://www.domesticworkers.org/about-us.

97 Randall K.Q. Akee, William E. Copeland, Gordon Keeler, Adrian Angold, and Elizabeth J. Costello, "Parents' Incomes and Children's Outcomes: A Quasi-Experiment," US National Library of Medicine National Institutes of Health, https://www.ncbi.nlm.nih.gov/pmc/articles/PMC2891175/.

98 "Visit to Buchenwald," Elie Wiesel Foundation for Humanity, September 25, 2017, http://eliewieselfoundation.org/news/visit-to-buchenwald/.

99 Sari Rosenberg, "October 13, 1970: Angela Davis Was Arrested, Setting off the 'Free Angela Davis' Campaign," *Lifetime,* October 13, 2017, https://www.mylifetime.com/she-did-that/october-13-1970-angela-davis-was-arrested-setting-off-the-free-angela-davis-campaign.

100 "Aretha Says She'll Go Angela's Bond if Permitted," *Jet Magazine,* December 3, 1970, https://books.google.com/books?id=njcDAAAAMBAJ&pg=PA54&lpg=PA54#v=onepage&q&f=false.

101   Lavanya Ramanathan, "Angela Davis is beloved, detested, misunderstood. What can a lifelong radical teach the resistance generation?" *Washington Post,* February 26, 2019, https://www.washingtonpost.com/lifestyle/style/ legendary-activist-angela-davis-has-overcome-doubters-her-whole-life--and -at-75-shes-still-not-backing-down/2019/02/26/87ffd4c0-3392-11e9-af5b -b51b7ff322e9_story.html?utm_term=.945e7f647f7e.

102   Ibid.

103   "Aretha Says She'll Go Angela's Bond if Permitted."

104   Ibid.

105   "Fanny Lou Hamer. 'We're On Our Way.' Speech Before a Mass Meeting Held at the Negro Baptist School in Indianola, Mississippi (September 1964)," Voices of Democracy, http://voicesofdemocracy.umd.edu/hamer -were-on-our-way-speech-text/.

106   "The Inauguration; Maya Angelou: 'On the Pulse of Morning,'" *New York Times,* January 21, 1993, https://www.nytimes.com/1993/01/21/us/the -inauguration-maya-angelou-on-the-pulse-of-morning.html.

107   Andrew Ross Sorkin, "Apple's Tim Cook Barnstorms for 'Moral Responsibility,'" *New York Times,* August 28, 2017, https://www.nytimes .com/2017/08/28/business/dealbook/tim-cook-apple-moral-responsibility .html.

108   "Transcript: Gov. Nikki Haley of South Carolina on Removing the Confederate Flag," *New York Times,* June 22, 2015, https://www.nytimes .com/interactive/2015/06/22/us/Transcript-Gov-Nikki-R-Haley-of-South -Carolina-Addresses-Removing-the-Confederate-Battle-Flag.html?mcubz=0.

109   "Mitch Landrieu's Speech on the Removal of Confederate Monuments in New Orleans," *New York Times,* May 23, 2017, https://www.nytimes .com/2017/05/23/opinion/mitch-landrieus-speech-transcript.html?mcubz=0.

110   Colin Campbell and Luke Broadwater, "Citing 'safety and security,' Pugh has Baltimore Confederate monuments taken down," *Baltimore Sun,* August 16, 2017, http://www.baltimoresun.com/news/maryland/baltimore-city/bs-md -ci-monuments-removed-20170816-story.html.

111   Amy B. Wang, "University of Texas takes down four Confederate statues overnight," *Washington Post,* August 21, 2017, https://www.washingtonpost .com/news/grade-point/wp/2017/08/21/university-of-texas-takes-down-four -confederate-statues-overnight/?utm_term=.862325dd98ab.

112   John Simons, "Where Are All the Black CEOs?" *Wall Street Journal,* May 21, 2018, https://www.wsj.com/articles/where-are-all-the-black-ceo-1526868360.

113   "Our History," Merck, https://www.merck.com/about/our-history/home .html.

114 Linda Villarosa, "Why America's Black Mothers and Babies Are in a Life-or-Death Crisis," *New York Times*, April 11, 2018, https://www.nytimes.com/2018/04/11/magazine/black-mothers-babies-death-maternal-mortality.html, "Pregnancy Associated Mortality," New York City Department of Health and Mental Hygiene Bureau of Maternal, Infant and Reproductive Health, https://www1.nyc.gov/assets/doh/downloads/pdf/ms/pregnancy-associated-mortality-report.pdf.

115 Desmond Tutu, *No Future Without Forgiveness* (New York: Doubleday, 1999), 218.

116 "Meet George W. Merck," Featured Stories, Merck, https://www.merck.com/about/our-people/george-merck.html.

117 Isaiah 58:10 New International Version, Bible Gateway, https://www.biblegateway.com/passage/?search=Isaiah+58%3A10&version=NIV.

118 Rev. Dr. William J. Barber, II, "We Need a Moral Breakthrough: Re. Dr. William J. Barber, II's Remarks to the URJ Biennial 2017," Union for Reformed Judaism, December 6, 2017, https://urj.org/blog/2017/12/06/we-need-moral-breakthrough-rev-dr-william-j-barber-iis-remarks-urj-biennial-2017.

119 Fox News (@FoxNews), Twitter post, August 8, 2017, https://twitter.com/FoxNews/status/894856213426356224.

120 Fox News, "Would you do that in front of the graves of the fallen," Facebook, https://www.facebook.com/watch/?v=10154567220981336.

121 Dinesh D'Souza, "Dinesh D'Souza: Colin Kaepernick's big lie," Fox News, September 25, 2017, http://www.foxnews.com/opinion/2017/09/25/dinesh-dsousza-colin-kaepernicks-big-lie.html.

122 Joe Walsh, "Colin Kaepernick is an un-American jackass," Facebook, October 14, 2016, https://www.facebook.com/joewalsh/posts/@%5b1458213354721 17:274:colin-kaepernick%5d-is-an-un/948361541935875/.

123 Rebecca Beatrice Brooks, "The Boston Tea Party," History of Massachusetts Blog, September 27, 2011, http://historyofmassachusetts.org/the-boston-tea-party/.

124 "Women of Protest: Photographs from the Records of the National Woman's Party," Library of Congress, https://www.loc.gov/teachers/classroommaterials/connections/women-protest/history3.html.

125 Fred Fay and Fred Pelka, "Justin Dart Obituary," *Ability Magazine,* June 22, 2002, https://abilitymagazine.com/JustinDart_remembered.html.

126 Ibid.

127 "October 2016 Donations," Kaepernick 7, Official Website, https://kaepernick7.com/blogs/million-dollar-pledge/k7-october-2016-donations.

128 Ibid.

129 Jane Coaston, "Nike Reignited the Kaepernick controversy in naming him the face of 'Just Do It,'" *Vox*, September 4, 2018, https://www.vox.com/2018/9/4/17818162/nike-kaepernick-controversy-face-of-just-do-it.

130 Andrew Carnegie, "The Gospel of Wealth."

131 Ibid.

132 Laura Arrillaga-Andreessen, *Giving 2.0* (Plano, TX: Jossey-Bass, 2012), https://books.google.com/books?id=8WwpKWioEtoC&pg=PT11&dq=%22anyone+who+gives+anything%22&hl=en&sa=X&ved=0ahUKEwimzsaEypfdAhVmdt8KHerSBgIQuwUILDAA#v=onepage&q=%22anyone%20who%20gives%20anything%22&f=false.

133 Michael F. Leonen, "Etiquette for Activists," *Yes Magazine*, May 20, 2004, https://www.yesmagazine.org/issues/a-conspiracy-of-hope/etiquette-for-activists.

134 MZ Many Names, "Attributing Words," Unnecessary Evils Blog, November 3, 2008, http://unnecessaryevils.blogspot.com/2008/11/attributing-words.html.

135 Ari Berman, "North Carolina's Moral Mondays," *The Nation*, July 17, 2013, https://www.thenation.com/article/north-carolinas-moral-mondays/.

136 Paul Blest, "Over 80,000 People Joined the Biggest-Ever Moral March in North Carolina," *The Nation*, February 13, 2017, https://www.thenation.com/article/over-80000-people-joined-the-biggest-ever-moral-march-in-north-carolina/, Cleve R. Wootson Jr., "Rev. William Barber builds a moral movement," *Washington Post*, June 29, 2017, https://www.washingtonpost.com/news/acts-of-faith/wp/2017/06/29/woe-unto-those-who-legislate-evil-rev-william-barber-builds-a-moral-movement/?utm_term=.76ca9b1f9dd2.

137 Cathy Lynn Grossman, "'Moral Monday' expands to a week of social justice action across U.S.," *Washington Post*, August 19, 2014, https://www.washingtonpost.com/national/religion/moral-monday-expands-to-a-week-of-social-justice-action-across-us/2014/08/19/27aec5d4-27e1-11e4-8b10-7db129976abb_story.html?utm_term=.ae8a390f621e, http://www.santafenewmexican.com/news/legislature/legislative-roundup-jan/article_c8be9dfb-e86c-5f0f-9294-401c82ac6ce6.html.

138 "Home," Poor People's Campaign, https://www.poorpeoplescampaign.org.

139 Tara Isabella Burton, "Poor People's Campaign rally revives Martin Luther King Jr.'s mission," *Vox*, https://www.vox.com/2018/6/22/17494070/poor-peoples-campaign-rally-revives-martin-luther-king-william-barber.

140 Sarah Ruiz-Grossman, "Sens. Warren, Sanders Hear Directly from America's Poor at U.S. Capitol," *Huffington Post*, June 12, 2018, https://www.huffingtonpost.com/entry/warren-sanders-cummings-poor-peoples-campaign_us_5b2048ece4b09d7a3d782673.

141 Ari Berman, "On the 50th Anniversary of the March on Washington, a New
     Civil Rights Movement Emerges," *The Nation,* August 24, 2013, https://www
     .thenation.com/article/50th-anniversary-march-washington-new-civil-rights
     -movement-emerges/, "Interview with Harry Belafonte," Interview, Eyes on
     the Prize Interviews, Washington University in St. Louis, May 15, 1989,
     http://digital.wustl.edu/e/eii/eiiweb/bel5427.0417.013harrybelafonte.html.

142 Joan Walsh, "The radical MLK we need today," *Salon,* January 20, 2014,
     https://www.salon.com/2014/01/20/the_radical_mlk_we_need_today/.

143 Jason L. Riley, "An Unsung Hero of Black Education," *Wall Street Journal,*
     December 22, 2015, https://www.wsj.com/articles/an-unsung-hero-of-black
     -education-1450829422.

144 Ibid.

145 Glenn A. Walsh, "The Carnegie Formula and Early Carnegie Libraries," May,
     1998, http://andrewcarnegie.tripod.com/carnformula.htm.

146 "Carnegie Libraries: The Future Made Bright," National Park Service
     U.S. Department of the Interior, https://www.nps.gov/nr/twhp/wwwlps/
     lessons/50carnegie/50carnegie.htm.

147 Rick Cohen, "The Challenge of Maintaining Andrew Carnegie's Library
     Legacy," *Nonprofit Quarterly,* July 10, 2013, https://nonprofitquarterly.org/
     2013/07/10/the-challenge-of-maintaining-andrew-carnegie-s-library-legacy/,
     Charles Strum, "Belleville Journal; Restoring Heritage and Raising
     the Future," *New York Times,* March 2, 1992, https://www.nytimes.com/
     1992/03/02/nyregion/belleville-journal-restoring-heritage-and-raising-hopes
     -for-future.html?src=pm.

148 Andrew Carnegie, "The Best Fields for Philanthropy," *The North American
     Review* 149, no. 397 (December 1889), https://www.jstor.org/stable/
     25101907?seq=1#metadata_info_tab_contents.

149 Andrew Carnegie, "The Gospel of Wealth."

150 Ibid.

151 Playboy Magazine, "'A Testament of Hope' by Dr. King," *Hef's Philosophy:
     Playboy and Revolution from 1965–1975,* accessed September 19, 2018,
     https://forthearticles.omeka.net/items/show/37.

152 Ibid.

153 Ibid.

ABOUT THE AUTHOR

Darren Walker is president of the Ford Foundation, a $16 billion international social justice philanthropy with offices in the United States and ten regions around the globe. Under his leadership, the Ford Foundation became the first nonprofit in US history to issue a $1 billion designated social bond in US capital markets for proceeds to strengthen and stabilize nonprofit organizations in the wake of Covid-19.

Before joining Ford, Darren was vice president at the Rockefeller Foundation, overseeing global and domestic programs including the Rebuild New Orleans initiative after Hurricane Katrina. In the 1990s, as COO of the Abyssinian Development Corporation—Harlem's largest community development organization—he led a comprehensive revitalization strategy, including building over a thousand units of affordable housing and the first major commercial development in Harlem since the 1960s. Earlier, he had a decade-long career in international law and finance at Cleary Gottlieb Steen & Hamilton and UBS.

Darren co-chairs New York City's Mayoral Advisory Commission on City Art, Monuments, and Markers, and serves on the Independent Commission on New York City Criminal Justice and Incarceration Reform and the UN International Labour Organization Global Commission on the Future of Work. He co-founded both the US Impact Investing Alliance and the

Presidents' Council on Disability Inclusion in Philanthropy and is a founding member of the Board Diversity Action Alliance. He chaired the philanthropy committee that brought a resolution to the city of Detroit's historic bankruptcy. He serves on many boards, including Lincoln Center for the Performing Arts, the National Gallery of Art, Carnegie Hall, the High Line, the Committee to Protect Journalists, and the Smithsonian National Museum of African American History and Culture. In the summer of 2020, he was appointed to the boards of Block, Inc., and Ralph Lauren. He is a member of the Council on Foreign Relations, the American Academy of Arts and Sciences, and the American Philosophical Society, and is the recipient of sixteen honorary degrees and university awards, including Harvard University's W.E.B. Du Bois Medal. In 2022, he was named Commander of the French Order of Arts and Letters, the nation's highest cultural honor, for his work as a benefactor of the arts. He was also appointed by Her Majesty, Queen Elizabeth II, to the Order of the British Empire for services to UK–US relations.

Educated exclusively in public schools, Darren was a member of the first class of Head Start in 1965 and received his bachelor's and law degrees from The University of Texas at Austin, which in 2009 recognized him with its Distinguished Alumnus Award—its highest alumni honor. He has been included on numerous leadership lists, including *TIME*'s annual 100 Most Influential People in the World, *Rolling Stone*'s 25 People Shaping the Future, *Fast Company*'s Most Creative People in Business, *Ebony*'s Power 100, and *Out* magazine's Power 50. Most recently, Darren was named *The Wall Street Journal*'s 2020 Philanthropy Innovator.

ABOUT THE
FORD FOUNDATION

The Ford Foundation is an independent organization working to address inequality and build a future grounded in justice. For more than eighty-five years, it has supported visionaries on the frontlines of social change worldwide, guided by its mission to strengthen democratic values, reduce poverty and injustice, promote international cooperation, and advance human achievement. Today, with an endowment of $16 billion, the foundation has headquarters in New York and ten regional offices across Africa, Asia, Latin America, and the Middle East.

ABOUT THE
FORD FOUNDATION

The Ford Foundation is an independent organization working to address inequality and build a future grounded in justice. For more than eighty-five years, it has supported visionaries on the frontlines of social change worldwide, guided by its mission to strengthen democratic values, reduce poverty and injustice, promote inte   onal cooperation, and advance human achievement.   ,, with an endowment of $16 billion, the foundation h   iquarters in New York and ten regional offices across   ica, Asia, Latin America, and the Middle East.